T0233977

Lecture Notes in Computer Science   **11225**

Commenced Publication in 1973
Founding and Former Series Editors:
Gerhard Goos, Juris Hartmanis, and Jan van Leeuwen

More information about this series at http://www.springer.com/series/7779

Per Stenström · Cristina Silvano · Koen Bertels
Michael Schulte (Eds.)

Transactions on High-Performance Embedded Architectures and Compilers V

 Springer

Editor-in-Chief
Per Stenström
Department of Computer Science
and Engineering
Chalmers University of Technology
Gothenburg, Sweden

Guest Editors
Cristina Silvano
Politecnico di Milano
Milan, Italy

Michael Schulte
University of Wisconsin–Madison
Madison, WI, USA

Koen Bertels
Delft University of Technology
Delft, The Netherlands

ISSN 0302-9743 ISSN 1611-3349 (electronic)
Lecture Notes in Computer Science
ISSN 1864-306X ISSN 1864-3078 (electronic)
Transactions on High-Performance Embedded Architectures and Compilers
ISBN 978-3-662-58833-8 ISBN 978-3-662-58834-5 (eBook)
https://doi.org/10.1007/978-3-662-58834-5

Library of Congress Control Number: 2019931832

This Springer imprint is published by the registered company Springer-Verlag GmbH, DE
part of Springer Nature
The registered company address is: Heidelberger Platz 3, 14197 Berlin, Germany

Guest Editorial

Special Issue on SAMOS 2009 International Symposium on Systems, Architectures, Modeling, and Simulation

SAMOS is a premier and well-established symposium on embedded computing systems organized annually since 2001. The symposium brings together highly qualified researchers from academia and industry on the quiet and inspiring northern mountainside of the Mediterranean island of Samos, one of the most beautiful islands of the Aegean. SAMOS offers an environment where collaboration rather than competition is fostered. In 2009, the SAMOS symposium comprised two co-located events:

- IC-SAMOS, IEEE International Conference on Embedded Computer Systems: Architectures, Modeling, and Simulation. The conference considers new state-of-the-art mature research papers on all aspects of embedded processor hardware/software design and integration. The IC-SAMOS is an IEEE co-sponsored conference (by both the IEEE CAS Society and the IEEE Germany SSCS chapter) and the conference proceedings are published in the IEEE series.
- SAMOS International Workshop on Systems, Architectures, Modeling, and Simulation, The workshop considers new state-of-the-art research papers as well as papers on ongoing work with promising preliminary results. Furthermore, the workshop covers special topics that are complementary to IC-SAMOS to cover challenging research trends. The workshop proceedings are published by Springer in the LNCS series.

The two events run in parallel and feature joint keynote presentations and social events. In 2009, the IC-SAMOS program included 23 research papers while the SAMOS Workshop enjoyed an interesting program of 18 research papers and 14 papers were included in three special sections organized on topics of current interests. All of the authors of the best paper award candidates for both IC-SAMOS and the SAMOS Workshop were later invited to submit an extended version of their work for consideration in this special issue. At the end of the review process, seven papers were selected for publication.

We would like to thank all reviewers for their rigorous work in reading and judging these papers: Their help and critical insight were invaluable for the selection process of this special issue. We would also like to thank the Editor-in-Chief Per Stenström for agreeing to provide space for this special issue and for accompanying us through all the steps of the process. To conclude, it is with great pleasure that we offer this selection to you, and we hope you can enjoy the reading and get inspiration for your future research works.

January 2019

Cristina Silvano
Koen Bertels
Michael Schulte

LNCS Transactions on High-Performance Embedded Architectures and Compilers

Editorial Board

Contents

Efficient Mapping of Streaming Applications for Image Processing
on Graphics Cards.   1
  Richard Membarth, Hritam Dutta, Frank Hannig, and Jürgen Teich

Programmable and Scalable Architecture for Graphics Processing Units.   21
  *Carlos S. de La Lama, Pekka Jääskeläinen, Heikki Kultala,
  and Jarmo Takala*

Circular Buffers with Multiple Overlapping Windows for Cyclic
Task Graphs.   39
  Tjerk Bijlsma, Marco J. G. Bekooij, and Gerard J. M. Smit

A Hardware-Accelerated Estimation-Based Power Profiling Unit - Enabling
Early Power-Aware Embedded Software Design and On-Chip
Power Management.   59
  *Andreas Genser, Christian Bachmann, Christian Steger,
  Reinhold Weiss, and Josef Haid*

The Abstract Streaming Machine: Compile-Time Performance Modelling
of Stream Programs on Heterogeneous Multiprocessors   79
  Paul M. Carpenter, Alex Ramirez, and Eduard Ayguade

Prototyping a Configurable Cache/Scratchpad Memory with Virtualized
User-Level RDMA Capability.   100
  *George Kalokerinos, Vassilis Papaefstathiou, George Nikiforos,
  Stamatis Kavadias, Xiaojun Yang, Dionisios Pnevmatikatos,
  and Manolis Katevenis*

A Dynamic Reconfigurable Super-VLIW Architecture for a Fault Tolerant
Nanoscale Design   121
  *Ricardo Ferreira, Cristoferson Bueno, Marcone Laure, Monica Pereira,
  and Luigi Carro*

Author Index   141

Efficient Mapping of Streaming Applications for Image Processing on Graphics Cards

Richard Membarth[1,2](✉) ⓘ, Hritam Dutta[3], Frank Hannig[4] ⓘ,
and Jürgen Teich[4] ⓘ

[1] DFKI GmbH, Saarland Informatics Campus, Saarbrücken, Germany
richard.membarth@dfki.de
[2] Saarland University, Saarland Informatics Campus, Saarbrücken, Germany
[3] Robert Bosch GmbH, Stuttgart, Germany
hritam.dutta@de.bosch.com
[4] Friedrich-Alexander University Erlangen-Nürnberg, Erlangen, Germany
{hannig,teich}@cs.fau.de

Abstract. In the last decade, there has been a dramatic growth in research and development of massively parallel commodity graphics hardware both in academia and industry. Graphics card architectures provide an optimal platform for parallel execution of many number crunching loop programs from fields like image processing or linear algebra. However, it is hard to efficiently map such algorithms to the graphics hardware even with detailed insight into the architecture. This paper presents a multiresolution image processing algorithm and shows the efficient mapping of this type of algorithms to graphics hardware as well as double buffering concepts to hide memory transfers. Furthermore, the impact of execution configuration is illustrated and a method is proposed to determine offline the best configuration. Using CUDA as programming model, it is demonstrated that the image processing algorithm is significantly accelerated and that a speedup of more than $145\times$ can be achieved on NVIDIA's Tesla C1060 compared to a parallelized implementation on a Xeon Quad Core. For deployment in a streaming application with steadily new incoming data, it is shown that the memory transfer overhead to the graphics card is reduced by a factor of six using double buffering.

Keywords: CUDA · OpenCL · Image processing ·
Mapping methodology · Streaming application

1 Introduction and Related Work

Nowadays noise reducing filters are employed in many fields like digital film processing or medical imaging to enhance the quality of images. These algorithms are computationally intensive and operate on single or multiple images. Therefore, dedicated hardware solutions have been developed in the past [2,4] in order

© Springer-Verlag GmbH Germany, part of Springer Nature 2019
P. Stenström et al. (Eds.): Transactions on HiPEAC V, LNCS 11225, pp. 1–20, 2019.
https://doi.org/10.1007/978-3-662-58834-5_1

to process images in real-time. However, with the overwhelming development of graphics processing units (GPUs) in the last decade, graphics cards became a serious alternative and were consequently deployed as accelerators for complex image processing far beyond simple rasterization [14].

In many fields, multiresolution algorithms are used to process a signal at different resolutions. In the JPEG 2000 and MPEG-4 standards, the discrete wavelet transform, which is also a multiresolution filter, is used for image compression [3,7]. Object recognition benefits from multiresolution filters as well by gaining scale invariance [5].

This paper presents a multiresolution algorithm for image processing and shows the efficient mapping of this type of algorithms to graphics hardware. The computationally intensive algorithm is accelerated on commodity graphics hardware and a performance superior to dedicated hardware solutions is achieved[1]. Furthermore, the impact of execution configuration is illustrated. A design space exploration is presented and a method is proposed to determine the best configuration. This is done offline and the information is used at run-time to achieve the best results on different GPUs. We consider not only the multiresolution algorithm on its own, but also its deployment in a application with repeated processing and data transfer phases: Instead of processing only one image, the algorithm is applied to a sequence of images transferred steadily one after the other into the graphics card. The transfer of the next image to the graphics card is overlapped with the processing of the current image using asynchronous memory transfers. We use the Compute Unified Device Architecture (CUDA) to implement the algorithm and application on GPUs from NVIDIA. The optimization principles and strategy, however, are not limited to CUDA, but are also valid for other frameworks like OpenCL [10].

This work is related to other studies. Ryoo et al. [13] present a performance evaluation of various algorithm implementations on the GeForce 8800 GTX. Their optimization strategy is, however, limited to compute-bound tasks. In another paper the same authors determine the optimal tile size by an exhaustive search [12]. Baskaran et al. [1] show that code could be generated for explicit managed memories in architectures like GPUs or the Cell processor that accelerate applications. However, they consider only optimizations for compute-bound tasks since these predominate. Similarly, none of them shows how to obtain the best configuration and performance on different graphics cards and they do not consider applications with overlapping data communication and processing phases at all. In comparison to our previous work in [9], support for applications employing double buffering concepts for overlapping computation and communication are also evaluated in this paper. The impact of hardware architecture changes of recent graphics card generations on the mapping strategy is also illustrated here.

---

[1] Exemplary, a comparison of the implementation in this work to the hardware solution in [4] for the bilateral filter kernel resulted in a speedup of 5× for an image of 1024 × 1024 with a filter window of 5 × 5 in terms of frames per second.

The remaining paper is organized as follows: Sect. 2 gives an overview of the hardware architecture. Subsequently, Sect. 3 illustrates the efficient mapping methodology for multiresolution applications employing double buffering to the graphics hardware. The application accelerated using CUDA is explained in Sect. 4, while Sect. 5 shows the results of mapping the algorithms and the application to the GPU. Finally, in Sect. 6, conclusions of this work are drawn.

2   Architecture

In this section, we present an overview of the Tesla C1060 architecture, which is used as accelerator for the algorithms studied within this paper. The Tesla is a highly parallel hardware platform with 240 processors integrated on a chip as depicted in Fig. 1. The processors are grouped into 30 streaming multiprocessors. These multiprocessors comprise eight scalar streaming processors. While the multiprocessors are responsible for scheduling and work distribution, the streaming processors do the calculations. For extensive transcendental operations, the multiprocessors also accommodate two special function units.

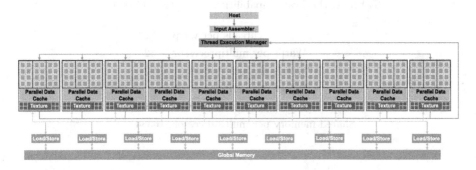

Fig. 1. Tesla architecture (cf. [11]): 240 streaming processors distributed over 30 multiprocessors. The 30 multiprocessors are partitioned into 10 groups, each comprising 3 multiprocessors, cache, and texture unit.

A program executed on the graphics card is called a *kernel* and is processed in parallel by many *threads* on the streaming processors. Therefore, each thread calculates a small portion of the whole algorithm, for example one pixel of a large image. A batch of these threads is always grouped together into a *thread block* that is scheduled to one multiprocessor and executed by its streaming processors. One of these thread blocks can contain up to 512 threads, which is specified by the programmer. The complete problem space has to be divided into sub-problems such that these can be processed independently within one thread block on one multiprocessor. The multiprocessor always executes a batch of 32 threads, also called a *warp*, in parallel. The two halves of a warp are sometimes further distinguished as *half-warps*. NVIDIA calls this new streaming multiprocessor architecture *single instruction, multiple thread* (SIMT) [8]. For all threads of a warp the same instructions are fetched and executed for each thread independently, that is, the threads of one warp can diverge and execute different branches. However, when this occurs the divergent branches are serialized until both branches merge again. Thereafter, the whole warp is executed in parallel again. This allows two forms of parallel processing on the graphics card, namely SIMD like processing within one thread block on the streaming processors and MIMD like processing of multiple thread blocks on the multiprocessors.

Each thread executed on a multiprocessor has full read/write access to the 4.0 GB *global memory* of the graphics card. This memory has, however, a long memory latency of 400 to 600 clock cycles. To hide this long latency each multiprocessor is capable to manage and switch between up to eight thread blocks, but not more than 1024 threads in total. In addition 16384 registers and 16384 bytes of on-chip *shared memory* are provided to all threads executed simultaneously on one multiprocessor. These memory types are faster than the global memory, but shared between all thread blocks executed on the multiprocessor. The capabilities of the Tesla architecture are summarized in Table 1.

Table 1. Hardware capabilities of the Tesla C1060.

Threads per warp	32
Warps per multiprocessor	32
Threads per multiprocessor	1024
Blocks per multiprocessor	8
Registers per multiprocessor	16384
Shared memory per multiprocessor	16384

Current graphics cards support also asynchronous data transfers between host memory and global memory. This allows to execute kernels on the graphics card, while data is transferred to or from the graphics card. Data transfers are handled like normal kernels and assigned to a queue of commands to be processed in order by the GPU. These queues are called *streams* in CUDA. Commands from different streams, however, can be executed simultaneously as long as one of the commands is a computational kernel and the other an asynchronous data transfer command. This provides support for double buffering concepts.

3   Mapping Methodology

To map applications efficiently to the graphics card, we propose a two-tiered approach. In the first step, we consider single applications separately, optimizing and mapping the algorithms of the application to the graphics hardware. Afterwards, we combine the individual applications on the GPU into one big application to hide memory transfers. The first step for single application mapping will be described at first, then double buffering support will be explained.

We distinguish between two types of kernels executed on the GPU, in order to map algorithms efficiently to graphics hardware. For each type a different optimization strategies applies. These are *compute-bound* and *memory-bound* kernels. While the execution time of compute-bound kernels is determined by the speed of the processors, for memory-bound kernels the limiting factor is the memory bandwidth. However, there are different measures to achieve a high throughput and good execution times for both kernel types. A flowchart of our proposed approach is shown in Fig. 2. First, for each task of the input application corresponding kernels are created. Afterwards, the memory access of these kernels is optimized and the kernels are added either to a compute-bound or memory-bound kernel set. Optimizations are applied to both kernel sets and the memory access pattern of the resulting kernels is again checked. Finally, the optimized kernels are obtained and the best configuration for each kernel is determined by a configuration space exploration.

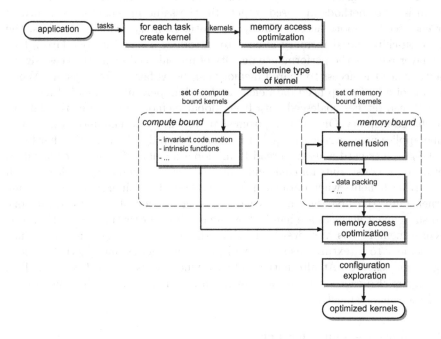

Fig. 2. Flowchart of proposed mapping strategy.

3.1   Memory Access

Although for both types of kernels different mapping strategies apply, a proper memory access pattern is necessary in all cases to achieve good memory transfer rates. Since all kernels get their data in the first place from global memory, reads and writes to this memory have to be *coalesced*. This means that all threads in both half-warps of the currently executed warp have to access contiguous elements in memory. For coalesced memory access, the access is combined to one memory transaction utilizing the entire memory bandwidth. Uncoalesced access needs multiple memory transactions instead and has a low bandwidth utilization. On older graphics cards like the Tesla C870, 16 separate memory transactions are issued for uncoalesced memory access instead of a single transaction resulting in a low bandwidth utilization. Also reading from global memory has a further restriction on these cards to achieve coalescing: The data accessed by the entire half-warp has to reside in the same segment of the global memory and has to be aligned to its size. For 32-bit and 64-bit data types the segment has a size of 64 bytes and 128 bytes, respectively. In contrast, newer graphics cards like the Tesla C1060 can combine all accesses within one segment to one memory transaction: Misaligned memory access require only one additional transaction, and the data elements do not need to reside contiguously in memory for achieving good bandwidth utilization.

Since many algorithms do not adhere to the constraints of the older graphics cards, two methods are used to get still the same memory performance as for coalesced memory access. Firstly, for both, memory reads and writes, the faster on-chip shared memory is used to introduce a new memory layer. This new layer reduces the performance penalty of uncoalesced memory access significantly since the access to shared memory can be as fast as for registers. When threads of a half-warp need data elements residing permuted in global memory, each thread fetches coalesced data from global memory and stores the data to the shared memory. Only reading from shared memory is then uncoalesced. The same applies when writing to global memory. Secondly, the texturing hardware of the graphics card is used to read from global memory. *Texture memory* does not have the constraints for coalescing. Instead, texture memory is cached, which has further benefits when data elements are accessed multiple times by the same kernel. Only the first data access has the long latency of the global memory and subsequent accesses are handled by the much faster texture cache. However, texture memory has also drawbacks since this memory is read-only and binding memory to a texture has some overhead. Nevertheless, most kernels benefit from using textures. An alternative to texture memory is *constant memory*. This memory is also cached and is used for small amounts of data when all threads read the same element.

3.2   Compute-Bound Kernels

Most algorithms that use graphics hardware as accelerator are computationally intensive and also the resulting kernels are limited by the performance of the streaming processors. To further accelerate these kernels—after optimizing the memory access—either the instruction count can be decreased or the time required by the instructions can be reduced. To reduce the instruction count traditional loop-optimization techniques can be adopted to kernels. For loop-invariant computationally intensive parts of a kernel it is possible to precalculate these offline and to retrieve these values afterwards from fast memory. This technique is also called *loop-invariant code motion* [16]. The precalculated values are stored in a lookup table, which may reside in texture or shared memory. Constant memory is chosen when all threads in a warp access the same element of the lookup table. The instruction performance issue is addressed by using intrinsic functions of the graphics hardware. These functions accelerate in particular transcendental functions like sine, cosine, and exponentiations at the expense of accuracy. Also other functions like division benefit from these intrinsics and can be executed in only 20 clock cycles instead of 32.

3.3   Memory-Bound Kernels

Compared to the previously described kernels, memory-bound kernels benefit from a higher ratio of arithmetic instructions to memory accesses. More instructions help to avoid memory stalls and to hide the long memory latency of global memory. Considering image processing applications, kernels operate on two-dimensional images that are processed typically using two nested loops on traditional CPUs. Therefore, *loop fusion* [16] can merge multiple kernels that operate on the same image as long as no inter-kernel data dependencies exist. Merging kernels provides often new opportunities for further code optimization. Another possibility to increase the ratio of arithmetic instructions to memory accesses is to calculate multiple output elements in each thread. This is true in particular when integers are used as data representation like in many image processing algorithms. For instance, the images considered for the algorithm presented next in this paper use a 10-bit grayscale representation. Therefore, only a fraction of the 4 bytes an integer occupies are needed. Because the memory hardware of GPUs is optimized for 4 byte operations, short data types yield inferior performance. However, data packing can be used to store two pixel values in the 4 bytes of an integer. Afterwards, integer operations can be used for memory access. Doing so increases also the ratio of arithmetic instructions to memory accesses.

3.4   Configuration Space Exploration

One of the basic principles when mapping a problem to the graphics card using CUDA is the tiling of the problem into smaller, independent sub-problems. This is necessary because only up to 512 threads can be grouped into one thread block. In addition, only threads of one block can cooperate and share data. Hence, proper tiling influences the performance of the kernel, in particular when intra-kernel dependencies prevail. The tiles can be specified in various ways, either one-, two-, or three-dimensional. The used dimension is such chosen that it maps directly to the problem, that is, two-dimensional tiles are used for image processing. The tile size has not only influence on the number of threads in a block and consequently how much threads in a block can cooperate, but also on the resource usage. Registers and shared memory are used by the threads of all scheduled blocks of one multiprocessor. Choosing smaller tiles allows a higher resource usage per thread on the one hand, while larger tiles support the cooperation of threads in a block on the other hand. Furthermore, the shape of a tile has influence on the memory access pattern and the memory performance, too. Consequently, it is not possible to give a formula that predicts the influence of the thread block configuration on the execution time. Therefore, configurations have to be explored in order to find the best configuration, although the amount of relevant configurations can be significantly narrowed down.

Since the hardware configuration varies for different GPUs, also the best block configuration changes. Therefore, we propose a method that allows to use always the best configuration for GPUs at run-time. We explore the configuration space for each graphics card model offline and store the result in a database. Later at run-time, the program identifies the model of the GPU and uses the configuration retrieved from the database. In that way there is no overhead at run-time and there is no penalty when a different GPU is used. In addition, the binary code size can be kept nearly as small as the original binary size.

3.5 Double Buffering Support

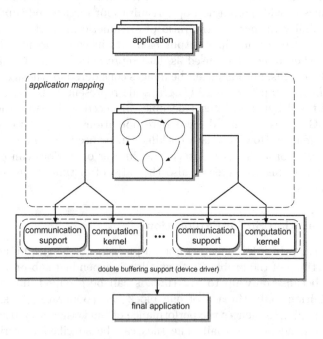

Fig. 3. Several independent applications are combined into one application employing double buffering concepts and the mapping strategy of Fig. 2.

The principle of overlapped computation and simultaneous data transfers is known as double or multi-buffering for architectures like the Cell Broadband

Engine, or graphics cards. This kind of overlapped kernel execution and data transfer is considered here to hide memory transfers. Most programs do not only consist of one single application executed once on the graphics card, but of several independent applications that have to be executed independently of each other. It is also possible that the same application has to be applied to different data, where the data is generated bit by bit (e. g., images are coming constantly from an external source). The previously introduced mapping strategy optimizes only the computation kernels, but does not consider a constant stream of data to be fed to the graphics card. The data has to be transferred every time over the PCI Express bus from the host. This data transfer requires a considerable amount of time compared to the time required to process the data. Newer graphics cards support, however, asynchronous data transfers and allow to transfer data to or from the graphics card while kernels are running. This way concepts like double buffering can be realized in order to hide the memory transfers to the graphics card. Figure 3 depicts a solution of how several independent applications can be combined to a single application with overlapping data transfers and data processing. Firstly, each application is mapped to and optimized for the graphics hardware as described in the mapping strategy of Fig. 2. This step gives us the computational kernels as well as the implicated communication support for these kernels. The kernels can now be scheduled in such a way that the data for one application streams to the graphics card while another algorithm is processed.

4   Multiresolution Filtering

The multiresolution application considered here utilizes the multiresolution approach presented by Kunz et al. [6] and employs a bilateral filter [15] as filter kernel. The application is a nonlinear multiresolution gradient adaptive filter for

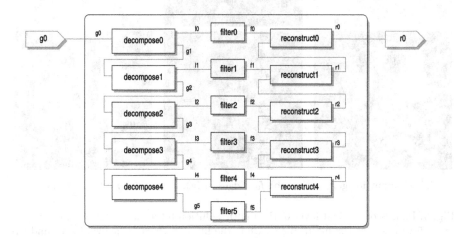

Fig. 4. Multiresolution filter application with five layers.

images and is typically used for intra-frame image processing, that is, only the information of one image is required. The filter reduces noise significantly while sharp image details are preserved. Therefore, the application uses a multiresolution approach representing the image at different resolutions so that each feature of the image can be processed on its most appropriate scale.

Figure 4 shows the used multiresolution application: In the decompose phase, two image pyramids with subsequently reduced resolutions ($g_0(1024 \times 1024)$, $g_1(512 \times 512)$, ... and $l_0(1024 \times 1024)$, $l_1(512 \times 512)$, ...) are constructed. While the images of the first pyramid (g_x) are used to construct the image of the next layer, the second pyramid (l_x) represents the edges in the image at different resolutions. The operations involved in these steps are to a large extent memory intensive with little computational complexity like upsampling, downsampling, or a lowpass operation. The actual algorithm of the application is working in the filter phase on the images produced by the decompose phase (l_0, ... l_4, g_5). This algorithm is described below in detail. After the main filter has processed these images, the output image is reconstructed again, reverting the steps of the decompose phase.

Figure 5 shows the images of the first layer of the multiresolution filter using a leaf as sample image (Fig. 5(a) is the input image g_0). The filtered edges of that image (f_0) are shown in Fig. 5(b) and the reconstructed image in Fig. 5(c). The output image is only smoothed at points where no edge is present.

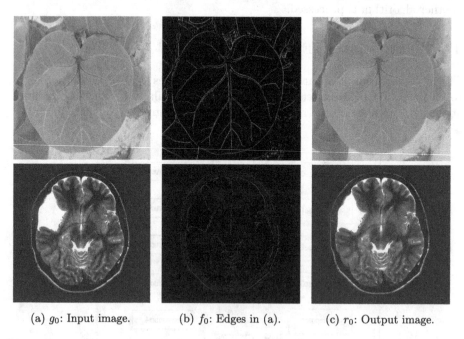

(a) g_0: Input image.   (b) f_0: Edges in (a).   (c) r_0: Output image.

Fig. 5. Images of the first layer of the multiresolution filter for a filter window of 5×5 ($\sigma_r = 5$): (a) shows the input image, while the filtered edges are shown in (b) and the final reconstructed image in (c).

The bilateral filter used in the filter phase of the multiresolution application applies the principle of traditional domain filters also to the range. Therefore, the filter has two components: One is operating on the domain of an image and considers the spatial vicinity of pixels, their *closeness*. The other component operates on the range of the image, that is, the vicinity refers to the *similarity* of pixel values. Closeness (Eq. (1)), hence, refers to geometric vicinity in the domain while similarity (Eq. (3)) refers to photometric vicinity in the range. We use Gaussian functions of the Euclidean distance for the closeness and similarity function as seen in Eqs. (2) and (4). The pixel in the center of the current filter window is denoted by x, whereas ξ denotes a point in the neighborhood of x. The function f is used to access the value of a pixel.

$$c(\xi, x) = e^{-\frac{1}{2}(\frac{d(\xi,x)}{\sigma_d})^2} \tag{1}$$

$$d(\xi, x) = d(\xi - x) = \|\xi - x\| \tag{2}$$

$$s(\xi, x) = e^{-\frac{1}{2}(\frac{\delta(f(\xi),f(x))}{\sigma_r})^2} \tag{3}$$

$$\delta(\phi, \widetilde{\phi}) = \delta(\phi - \widetilde{\phi}) = \|\phi - \widetilde{\phi}\| \tag{4}$$

The bilateral filter replaces each pixel by an average of geometric nearby and photometric similar pixel values as described in Eq. (5) with the normalizing function of Eq. (6). Only pixels within the neighborhood of the relevant pixel are used. The neighborhood and consequently also the kernel size is determined by the geometric spread σ_d. The parameter σ_r (photometric spread) in the similarity function determines the amount of combination. When the difference of pixel values is less than σ_r, these values are combined, otherwise not.

$$h(x) = k^{-1}(x) \int_{-\infty}^{\infty} \int_{-\infty}^{\infty} f(\xi)c(\xi, x)s(f(\xi), f(x)) \, d\xi \tag{5}$$

$$k(x) = \int_{-\infty}^{\infty} \int_{-\infty}^{\infty} c(\xi, x)s(f(\xi), f(x)) \, d\xi \tag{6}$$

Compared to the memory access dominated decompose and reconstruct phases, the bilateral filter is compute intensive. Considering a 5×5 filter kernel ($\sigma_d = 1$), 50 exponentiations are required for each pixel of the image—25 for each, the closeness and similarity function. While the mask coefficients for the closeness function are static, those for the similarity function have to be calculated dynamically based on the photometric vicinity of pixel values.

Algorithm 1 shows exemplarily the implementation of the bilateral filter on the graphics card. For each pixel of the output image, one thread is used to apply the bilateral filter. These threads are grouped into thread blocks and process partitions of the image. All blocks together process the whole image. While the threads within one block execute in SIMD, different blocks execute in MIMD on the graphics hardware.

Algorithm 1. Bilateral filter implementation on the graphics card.

```
 1  forall thread blocks B do in parallel
 2      for each thread t in thread block b do in parallel
 3          x, y ← get_global_index(b, t);
 4          for yf = −2 ∗ sigma_d to+2 ∗ sigma_d do
 5              for xf = −2 ∗ sigma_d to+2 ∗ sigma_d do
 6                  c ← closeness((x, y), (x + xf, y + yf));
 7                  s ← similarity(input [x, y], input [x + xf, y + yf]);
 8                  k ← k + c ∗ s;
 9                  p ← p + c ∗ s ∗ input[x + xf, y + yf];
10              end
11          end
12          output[x][y] ← p/k;
13      end
14  end
```

---

5 Results

This section shows the results when the described mapping strategy of Sect. 3 is applied to the multiresolution filter implementation and double buffering support is added to process a sequence of images. We show the improvements that we attain for compute-bound kernels as well as memory-bound kernels. Furthermore, our proposed method for optimal configuration is shown exemplarily for a Tesla C1060 and a GeForce 8400.

For the compute-bound bilateral filter kernel, loop-invariant code is precalculated and stored in lookup tables. This is done for the closeness function as well as for the similarity function. In addition, texture memory is used to improve the memory performance. Aside from global memory, linear texture memory as well as a two-dimensional texture array are considered. Figure 6(a) shows the impact of the lookup tables and texture memory on the execution time for the older Tesla C870. The lookup tables are stored in constant memory. First, it can be seen that textures reduce significantly the execution times, in particular when linear texture memory is used. The biggest speedup is gained using a lookup table for the closeness function while the speedup for the similarity function is only marginal. Using lookup tables for both functions provides no further improvement. In the closeness function all threads access the same element of the lookup table. Since the constant memory is optimized for such access patterns, this lookup table shows the biggest gain in acceleration. In Fig. 6(b) intrinsic functions are used in addition. Compiling a program with the *-use_fast_math* compiler option enables intrinsic functions for the whole program. In particular the naïve implementation benefits from this, having most arithmetic operations of all implementations. Altogether, the execution time is reduced more than 66% for processing the best implementation using a lookup table for the closeness function as well as intrinsic functions. This implementation achieves

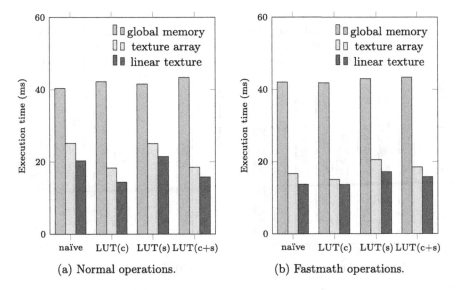

Fig. 6. Optimization of the compute-bound bilateral filter (filter window size: 9×9) kernel on the Tesla C870: Shown is the influence of loop-invariant code motion and intrinsic functions for an image of 1024×1024 using different memory types on the execution time for processing a single image. (a) shows the results for normal arithmetic operations and (b) using *fastmath* operations.

up to 63 GFLOPS counting a lookup table access as one operation. For the naïve implementation over 113 GFLOPS are achieved using intrinsic functions.

Using the same configuration for the newer Tesla C1060 shows the influence of the newer memory abstraction level: Global memory has almost the same performance as texture memory as seen in Fig. 7(a). Still, linear texture memory and texture arrays are faster, but only marginal, compared to older graphics cards. Figure 7(b) shows that using intrinsic functions reduces the execution times further. The best result is achieved here using a texture array and intrinsic functions being 51% faster and obtaining up to 149 GFLOPS. For the naïve implementation over 225 GFLOPS are achieved using intrinsic functions.

The kernels for the decompose and reconstruct phases are memory-bound. Initially for each task of these phases a separate kernel is used, that is, one kernel for lowpass filtering, upsampling, downsampling, etc. Subsequently these kernels are fused as long as data dependencies are met. Figure 8 shows the impact of merging kernels exemplarily for a sequence of tasks, which is further called *expand* operator: First, the image is upsampled, then a lowpass filter is applied to the resulting image and finally the values are multiplied by a factor of four. This operator is used in the decompose phase as well as in the reconstruct phase. Merging the kernels for these tasks reduces global memory accesses and allows further optimizations within the new kernel. The execution time for an input image of 512×512 (i.e., upsampling to 1024×1024 and processing at

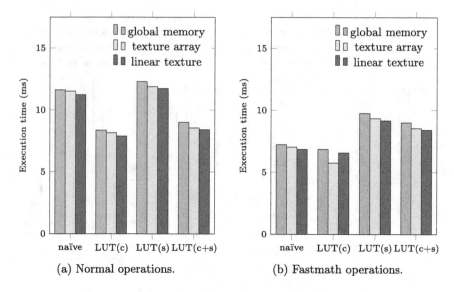

Fig. 7. Optimization of the compute-bound bilateral filter (filter window size: 9×9) kernel on the Tesla C1060: Shown is the influence of loop-invariant code motion and intrinsic functions for an image of 1024×1024 using different memory types on the execution time for processing a single image. (a) shows the results for normal arithmetic operations and (b) using *fastmath* operations.

this resolution) could be significantly reduced from about 4.70 ms (1.04 ms) to 0.67 ms (0.14 ms) for the Tesla C870 (Tesla C1060). However, writing the results back to global memory of the new kernel is uncoalesced since each thread has to write two consecutive data elements after the upsampling step. Therefore, shared memory is used to buffer the results of all threads and write them afterwards coalesced back to global memory. This reduces the execution time further to 0.18 ms (0.10 ms). The performance of the expand operator was improved by 96% and 90%, respectively, using kernel fusion.

After the algorithm is mapped to the graphics hardware, the thread block configuration is explored. The configuration space for two-dimensional tiles comprises 3280 possible configurations. Since always 16 elements have to be accessed in a row for coalescing, only such configurations are considered. This reduces the number of relevant configurations to 119, 3.6% of the whole configuration space. From these configurations, we assumed that a square block with 16×16 threads would yield the best performance for the bilateral filter kernel. Because each thread loads also its neighboring pixels, a square block configuration utilizes the texture cache best when loading data. However, the exploration shows that the best configurations have 64×1 threads on the Tesla C1060, 16×6 on the Tesla C870, and 32×6 on the GeForce 8400. Figures 9 and 10 show the execution times of the 119 considered configurations exemplarily for the Tesla C1060 and the GeForce 8400. The data set is plotted in 2D for better visualization. Plotted

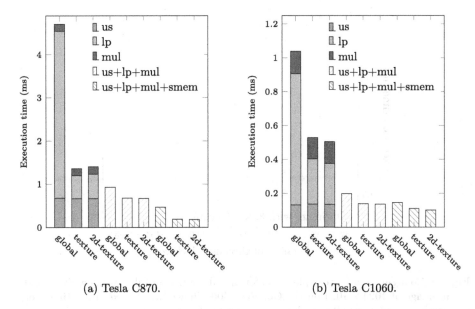

(a) Tesla C870.   (b) Tesla C1060.

Fig. 8. Optimization of the memory-bound expand operator: Shown is the influence of merging multiple kernels (upsampling (us), lowpass (lp), and multiplication (mul)) and utilization of shared memory (smem) to achieve coalescing for an input image of 512×512 (i.e., upsampled to and processed at 1024×1024). Note: The scale is different for the two graphs.

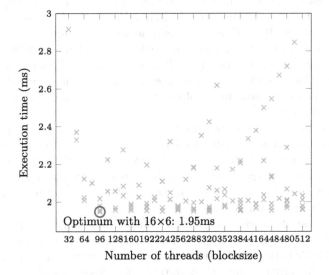

Fig. 9. Configuration space exploration for the bilateral filter (filter window size: 5×5) for an image of 1024×1024 on the Tesla C1060. Shown are the execution times for processing the bilateral filter in dependence on the blocksize.

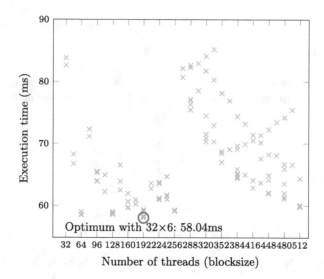

Fig. 10. Configuration space exploration for the bilateral filter (filter window size: 5×5) for an image of 1024 × 1024 on the GeForce 8400. Shown are the execution times for processing the bilateral filter in dependence on the blocksize.

against the x-axis are the number of threads of the block. That is, the configuration 16×16 and 32×8 have for instance the same x-value. The best configuration takes 1.95 ms on the Tesla C1060, 4.19 ms on the Tesla C870, and 58.04 ms on the GeForce 8400, whereas the previously as optimal assumed configuration of 16 × 16 takes 1.98 ms, 4.67 ms, and 59.22 ms. While the best configuration is 10.3% faster on the Tesla C870, it is only about 2% faster on the other two cards. Compared to the worst (however coalesced) configuration the best configuration is more than 50% faster in all cases. While the best configuration is fixed for a workload utilizing all resources on the graphics card, the optimal configuration changes when the graphics card is only partially utilized (e. g., for an image of 64 × 64).

This shows that the best configuration for an application is not predictable and that an exploration is needed to determine the best configuration for each graphics card. These configurations are determined once offline and stored to a database. Later at run-time, the application has only to load its configuration from the database. This way always the best performance can be achieved with only a moderate code size increase.

A comparison of the complete multiresolution filter implementation with a CPU implementation shows the speedup that can be achieved on current graphics cards. The CPU implementation uses the same optimizations as the implementation on the graphics card (lookup tables for closeness and similarity functions). OpenMP is used to utilize all four cores of the used Xeon Quad Core E5430 (2.66 GHz) and scales almost linear with the number of cores. On the graphics cards and CPU, the best performing implementations are chosen. As seen in Table 2, the Tesla C1060 achieves a speedup between 66× for small images and 145× for large images compared to the Quad Core. Images up to a resolution of 2048 × 2048 can be processed in real-time using a filter window of 9 × 9, while not even images of 512 × 512 can be processed in real-time on the CPU. None of the optimizations change the algorithm itself, but improve the performance. Only when using fastmath, the floating point intermediate results of the bilateral filter differ slightly. This has, however, no impact on the output image or on the quality of the image. If the accuracy of floating point number representation is not required, good performance can be achieved using fastmath with minimal programming effort.

Table 2. Speedup and frames per second (FPS) for the multiresolution application on a Tesla C1060 and a Xeon Quad Core (2.66 GHz) for a filter window size of 9 × 9 and different image sizes.

	512 × 512	1024 × 1024	2048 × 2048	4096 × 4096
FPS (Xeon)	4.58	1.01	0.19	0.005
FPS (Tesla)	306.55	97.05	26.19	0.66
Speedup	66.95	89.11	135.62	145.88

To support double buffering, we use different CUDA *streams* to process one image while the next image is transferred to the graphics memory. Figure 11 shows the activity of the two streams used to realize double buffering in a Gantt chart. The first image has to be on hand before the two streams can use asynchronous data transfers to hide the data transfers of the successive iterations. Each command in a stream is denoted by an own box showing the layered approach of the multiresolution filter. The data was acquired during profiling where each asynchronous data transfer did not overlap with kernel execution as seen in the Gantt chart. Using the double buffering implementation, most of the data transfers can be hidden as seen in Table 3. The execution time of 100 iterations with no data transfers takes about 133 ms. Using only one stream and synchronous memory transfers takes about 166 ms, hence, 33 ms are required for the data transfers. Using asynchronous memory transfers, the 100 iterations take 138 ms, only 5 ms instead of 33 ms for the data transfers.

Table 3. Execution time for 100 iterations of the multiresolution filter application for different memory management approaches when no X–server is running.

No data transfers	133.61 ms
Synchronous memory transfers	166.28 ms
Asynchronous memory transfers	138.28 ms

Fig. 11. Gantt chart of the multiresolution filter employing double buffering, process-ing five images. Two streams are used for asynchronous memory transfers. While one stream transfers the next image to the graphics memory, the current image is processed on the graphics card. Red boxes denote asynchronous memory transfers while kernel execution is denoted by blue boxes. (Color figure online)

6 Conclusions

In this paper it has been shown that multiresolution filters can leverage the potential of current highly parallel graphics cards hardware using CUDA. The image processing algorithm was accelerated by more than one order of magni-tude. Whether a task is compute-bound or memory-bound, different approaches have been presented in order to achieve remarkable speedups. Memory-bound tasks benefit from a higher ratio of arithmetic instructions to memory accesses, whereas for compute-bound kernels the instruction count has to be decreased at the expense of additional memory accesses. Finally, it has been shown how the best configuration for kernels can be determined by exploration of the configu-ration space. To avoid exploration at run-time for different graphics cards the best configuration is determined offline and stored in a database. At run-time the application retrieves the configuration for its card from the database. That way, the best performance can be achieved independent of the used hardware.

Applying this strategy to a multiresolution application with a computation-ally intensive filter kernel yielded remarkable speedups. The implementation on the Tesla outperformed an optimized and also parallelized CPU implementation on a Xeon Quad Core by a factor of up to 145. The computationally most inten-sive part of the multiresolution application achieved over 225 GFLOPS taking advantage of the highly parallel architecture. The configuration space explo-ration for the kernels revealed more than 10% faster configurations compared to configurations thought to be optimal. Using double buffering to hide the mem-ory transfer times, the data transfer overhead was reduced by a factor of six. An implementation of the multiresolution filter as gimp plugin is also available online[2] showing the impressive speedup compared to conventional CPUs.

---

[2] https://www12.cs.fau.de/people/membarth/cuda/.

Acknowledgments. We are indebted to our colleagues Philipp Kutzer and Michael Glaß for providing the sample pictures.

References

1. Baskaran, M., Bondhugula, U., Krishnamoorthy, S., Ramanujam, J., Rountev, A., Sadayappan, P.: Automatic data movement and computation mapping for multi-level parallel architectures with explicitly managed memories. In: Proceedings of the 13th ACM SIGPLAN Symposium on Principles and Practice of Parallel Programming, pp. 1–10. ACM, February 2008. https://doi.org/10.1145/1345206.1345210
2. do Carmo Lucas, A., Ernst, R.: An image processor for digital film. In: Proceedings of IEEE 16th International Conference on Application-Specific Systems, Architectures, and Processors (ASAP), pp. 219–224. IEEE, July 2005. https://doi.org/10.1109/ASAP.2005.13
3. Christopoulos, C., Skodras, A., Ebrahimi, T.: The JPEG2000 still image coding system: an overview. Trans. Consum. Electron. **46**(4), 1103–1127 (2000). https://doi.org/10.1109/30.920468
4. Dutta, H., Hannig, F., Teich, J., Heigl, B., Hornegger, H.: A design methodology for hardware acceleration of adaptive filter algorithms in image processing. In: Proceedings of IEEE 17th International Conference on Application-Specific Systems, Architectures, and Processors (ASAP), pp. 331–337. IEEE, September 2006. https://doi.org/10.1109/ASAP.2006.4
5. Kemal Ekenel, H., Sankur, B.: Multiresolution face recognition. Image Vis. Comput. **23**(5), 469–477 (2005). https://doi.org/10.1016/j.imavis.2004.09.002
6. Kunz, D., Eck, K., Fillbrandt, H., Aach, T.: Nonlinear multiresolution gradient adaptive filter for medical images. In: Proceedings of the SPIE: Medical Imaging 2003: Image Processing, vol. 5032, pp. 732–742. SPIE, May 2003. https://doi.org/10.1117/12.481323
7. Li, W.: Overview of fine granularity scalability in MPEG-4 video standard. Trans. Circuit. Syst. Video Technol. **11**(3), 301–317 (2001). https://doi.org/10.1109/76.911157
8. Lindholm, E., Nickolls, J., Oberman, S., Montrym, J.: NVIDIA Tesla: a unified graphics and computing architecture. IEEE Micro **28**(2), 39–55 (2008). https://doi.org/10.1109/MM.2008.31
9. Membarth, R., Hannig, F., Dutta, H., Teich, J.: Efficient mapping of multiresolution image filtering algorithms on graphics processors. In: Bertels, K., Dimopoulos, N., Silvano, C., Wong, S. (eds.) SAMOS 2009. LNCS, vol. 5657, pp. 277–288. Springer, Heidelberg (2009). https://doi.org/10.1007/978-3-642-03138-0_31
10. Munshi, A.: The OpenCL Specification. Khronos OpenCL Working Group (2009)
11. Owens, J., Houston, M., Luebke, D., Green, S., Stone, J., Phillips, J.: GPU computing. Proc. IEEE **96**(5), 879–899 (2008). https://doi.org/10.1109/JPROC.2008.917757
12. Ryoo, S., Rodrigues, C., Stone, S., Baghsorkhi, S., Ueng, S., Hwu, W.: Program optimization study on a 128-core GPU. In: The First Workshop on General Purpose Processing on Graphics Processing Units (GPGPU) (2007)

13. Ryoo, S., Rodrigues, C., Baghsorkhi, S., Stone, S., Kirk, D., Wen-Mei, W.: Optimization principles and application performance evaluation of a multithreaded GPU using CUDA. In: Proceedings of the 13th ACM SIGPLAN Symposium on Principles and Practice of Parallel Programming (PPoPP), pp. 73–82. ACM, February 2008. https://doi.org/10.1145/1345206.1345220

14. Stone, S., Haldar, J., Tsao, S., Wen-Mei, W., Liang, Z., Sutton, B.: Accelerating advanced MRI reconstructions on GPUs. In: Proceedings of the 2008 Conference on Computing Frontiers, pp. 261–272, October 2008. https://doi.org/10.1016/j.jpdc.2008.05.013

15. Tomasi, C., Manduchi, R.: Bilateral filtering for gray and color images. In: Proceedings of the Sixth International Conference on Computer Vision, pp. 839–846, January 1998. https://doi.org/10.1109/ICCV.1998.710815

16. Wolfe, M., Shanklin, C., Ortega, L.: High Performance Compilers for Parallel Computing. Addison-Wesley Longman Publishing Co., Boston (1995)

Programmable and Scalable Architecture for Graphics Processing Units

Carlos S. de La Lama[1]([✉]) [iD], Pekka Jääskeläinen[2] [iD], Heikki Kultala[2] [iD], and Jarmo Takala[2] [iD]

[1] Department of Computer Architecture, Computer Science and Artificial Intelligence, Universidad Rey Juan Carlos, Móstoles, Spain
carlos.delalama@urjc.es
[2] Tampere University, Tampere, Finland
{pekka.jaaskelainen,heikki.kultala,jarmo.takala}@tuni.fi

Abstract. Graphics processing is an application area with high level of parallelism at the data level and at the task level. Therefore, graphics processing units (GPU) are often implemented as multiprocessing systems with high performance floating point processing and application specific hardware stages for maximizing the graphics throughput.

In this paper we evaluate the suitability of Transport Triggered Architectures (TTA) as a basis for implementing GPUs. TTA improves scalability over the traditional VLIW-style architectures making it interesting for computationally intensive applications. We show that TTA provides high floating point processing performance while allows more programming freedom than vector processors.

Finally, one of the main features of the presented TTA-based GPU design is its fully programmable architecture making it a suitable target for general purpose computing on GPU APIs which have become popular in the recent years.

Keywords: GPU · GPGPU · TTA · VLIW · GLSL · OpenGL · OpenCL

1 Introduction

3D graphics processing can be seen as a compound of sequential stages applied to a set of input data. Commonly, graphics processing systems are abstracted as so called *graphics pipelines* with only minor differences between the various existing APIs and implementations. Therefore, *stream processing* [30], where a number of kernels (user defined or fixed) are applied to a stream of data of the same type, is often thought as the computing paradigm of graphics processing units.

Early 3D accelerating GPUs were essentially designed to perform a fixed set of operations in an effective manner, with no capabilities to customize this process [4]. Later, some vendors started to add programmability to their GPU

© Springer-Verlag GmbH Germany, part of Springer Nature 2019
P. Stenström et al. (Eds.): Transactions on HiPEAC V, LNCS 11225, pp. 21–38, 2019.
https://doi.org/10.1007/978-3-662-58834-5_2

products, leading to standardization of "shading languages". Both of the major graphics APIs (OpenGL and DirectX) provided their own implementation of such languages. DirectX introduced the *High Level Shading Language* [29], while OpenGL defined the *OpenGL Shading Language* (GLSL) [10], first supported as an optional extension to OpenGL 1.4 and later becoming part of the standard in OpenGL 2.0. Each new version of the standard has increased the capabilities of the language.

GLSL is similar to the standard C language, but includes some additional data types for vectors and matrices, and library functions to perform the common operations with the data types. Programs written in GLSL (called *shaders*) can customize the behavior of specific stages of the OpenGL graphics pipeline (dashed boxes in Fig. 1) [16].

Vertex shaders are applied to the input points defining the vertices of the graphics primitives (such as points, lines or polygons) in a 3D coordinate system called *model space*.

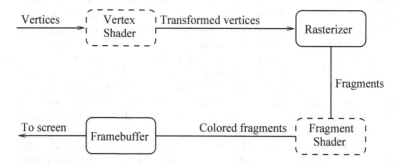

Fig. 1. Simplified view of the customizable OpenGL pipeline.

Depending on the type of primitive being drawn, the rasterizer then generates a number of visible points between the transformed vertices. These new points are called *fragments*. Each drawn primitive usually produces a number of fragments equal to the screen pixels it covers. The rasterizer interpolates several attributes, such as color or texture coordinates, between vertices to find the corresponding value (called *varying*) for each fragment, and the programmable *fragment shader* can postprocess and modify those values.

In OpenGL 3.2, yet another shader type was introduced. *Geometry shaders* that are executed after vertex shaders modify primitives as entities. They are not considered in this paper, but adding support for them in our software pipeline should be straightforward.

The great computing power present in the graphic devices led to the use of shaders to perform general purpose calculations (GPGPU) [23]. This way of exploiting the GPU's computation resources posed additional challenges as every algorithm had to be mapped to the shader language's datatypes and functions that were not designed for non-graphics computation. As a consequence,

GPU vendors started providing APIs for easier non-graphics programming of the processors, giving birth to the era of "GPU Computing" [22]. Finally, in the end of 2008, a vendor-neutral API for programming heterogeneous platforms (which can include also GPU-like resources) was standardized. The OpenCL standard [11] was welcomed by the GPGPU community as a generic alternative to platform-specific APIs such as NVIDIA's CUDA [6].

Using languages such as GLSL, OpenCL or CUDA, programmers can harness all the computing power of graphic devices for running highly parallelizable algorithms. However, while these languages closely resemble high level programming languages (HLL), some of the complex conditional constructs are either not supported, or discouraged as they would cause a great performance degradation on currently popular GPU hardware which execute instances of parallel kernels as single-instruction multiple-data (SIMD) instruction elements [15,17].

In this paper we propose a programmable and scalable GPU architecture called TTAGPU which implements almost all of the graphics pipeline in software. The full programmability allows it to be adapted for GPGPU style of computation, and, for example, to support the OpenCL API [9]. Our approach exploits parallelism at the instruction level, thus avoids the programming freedom degradation caused by the SIMD programming model.

The paper extends our previous work in [12], adding additional considerations on the advantages of the proposed solution over widespread GPU architectures and additional benchmarks.

The rest of the paper is organized as follows. Section 2 discusses briefly the related work, Sect. 3 describes the main points in the TTAGPU design, Sect. 4 gives an overview to the software implementation of the TTAGPU graphics pipeline, Sect. 5 provides some results on the floating point scalability of the architecture and compares against an existing SPMD-based GPU, and Sect. 6 concludes the paper and discusses the future directions.

2   Related Work

The first generation of programmable GPUs included specialized hardware for vertex processing and fragment processing as separate components, together with texture mapping units and rasterizers, set up on a multi-way stream configuration to exploit the inherent parallelism present on 3D graphic algorithms [19].

As modern applications needed to customize the graphic processing to a higher degree, it became obvious that such heterogeneous architectures were not the ideal choice. Therefore, with the appearance of the *unified shader model* in 2007 [14], the differences between vertex and fragment shaders begun to disappear. Newer devices have a number of *unified shaders* that can do the same arithmetic operations and access the same buffers (although some differences in the instruction sets are still present). This provides better programmability to the graphic pipeline, while the fixed hardware on critical parts (like the rasterizer) ensures high performance. However, the stream-like connectivity between computing resources still limits the customization of the processing algorithm. The major GPU vendors (NVIDIA & ATI) follow this approach in their latest products [32,33].

The performance of the unified shader is evaluated in [18] by means of implementing a generic GPU microarchitecture and simulating it. The main conclusion of the paper is that although graphics rendering performance improves only marginally with respect to non-unified shader architectures, it has real benefits in terms of efficiency per area.

NVIDIA architecture called Fermi introduced some interesting new features over previous GPUs from the vendor [21]. The most advertised features in Fermi are geared towards a better support for legacy high level languages such as C++. However, the architecture is still based on the SPMD programming model, thus suffers from the same programming freedom restrictions as the earlier architectures.

A different approach to achieve GPU flexibility is being proposed by Intel with its Larrabee processor [27]. Instead of starting from a traditional GPU architecture, they propose an x86-compatible device with additional floating point units for enhanced arithmetic performance. Larrabee includes very little specific hardware, the most notable exception being the texture mapping unit. Instead, the graphics pipeline is implemented in software, making it easier to modify and customize. Larrabee is to be deployed as a "many-core" solution, with number of cores in 64 and more. Each core comprises a 512-bit vector FPU capable of 16 simultaneous single-precision floating point operations. At the end of 2009, Intel announced a significant delay in the deployment of the first Larrabee devices. GPUs based on it are not at the moment being released for consumer products, but only for some developers. While the reasons behind this move are not known at the time of this writing (mid 2010), one common rumour is the software renderer not reaching the expected performance figures.

The solution we propose also implements the graphics pipeline in software, but the underlying processor architecture is completely different from Larrabee. A major difference is that TTAGPU is not tied to the x86 instruction set architecture (ISA). As there is no legacy instruction support burden in TTAGPU the chip area can be used for operations that better suit the demands of graphics workloads. Another difference is x86 ISA's lack of static instruction level parallelism (ILP). In order for Larrabee to exploit more general ILP on top of the data level parallelism of its additional vector instructions, it would need runtime scheduling hardware that complicates the microarchitecture of a single core.

3   TTAGPU Architecture

The goal of the TTAGPU design is to implement an OpenGL-compliant graphics API which is executed on a customized TTA processor, supports customization of the graphic pipeline as described in the OpenGL specification [26] and allows general-purpose programming with support for OpenCL API. Ideally, TTAGPU should be capable of running the graphics pipeline at a speed comparable to fixed hardware alternatives with the same function unit and register resources while maintaining full programmability for wider API support. The single core of TTAGPU is a TTA processor tailored with the appropriate function units to obtain near-optimum performance when running a software implementation of the graphic pipeline.

3.1 Transport Triggered Architectures

VLIWs are considered interesting processor alternatives for applications with high requirements for data processing performance [1] and with limited control flow, such as graphics processing. Transport Triggered Architectures (TTA) is a modular processor architecture template with high resemblance to VLIW architectures. The main difference between TTAs and VLIWs can be seen in how they are programmed: instead of defining which operations are started in which function units at which instruction cycles, TTA programs are defined as data transports between register files (RF) and FUs of the datapath. The operations are started as side-effects of writing operand data to the "triggering port" of the FU. Figure 2 presents a simple example TTA processor [2].

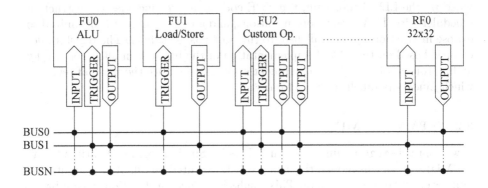

Fig. 2. Example of a TTA processor.

The programming model of VLIW imposes limitations for scaling the number of FUs in the datapath. Increasing the number of FUs has been problematic in VLIWs due to the need to include as many write and read ports in the RFs as there are FU operations potentially accessing it the same time. Additional ports increase the RF complexity, resulting in larger area, critical path delay and power consumption. In case the VLIW supports register file bypassing, adding an FU to the datapath requires new bypassing paths to be added from the FU's output ports to the input ports of the other FUs, increasing the interconnection network complexity. Thanks to its programmer-visible interconnection network, TTA datapath can support more FUs with simpler RFs [3]. Because the timing of data transports between datapath units are programmer-defined, there is no obligation to scale the number of RF ports according to the worst case number of

FUs accessing the RF at the same time [7]. As the register file bypassing is done in software instead of hardware, it is often possible to avoid the use of general purpose registers as temporary storage, thus reducing both register pressure and register file port requirements even further. In addition, as the datapath connectivity is part of the architecture (visible to the programmer), it can be tailored according to the set of applications at hand, including only the connections that benefit the application the most. The connectivity customization can be done in such a way that the connectivity is optimized to a set of applications while preserving enough connectivity for full programmability with potential performance penalty for the non-optimized programs due to extra register copy moves.

In order to support fast automated design of TTA processors, a toolset project called TTA-based Codesign Environment (TCE) was started in 2003 in Tampere University of Technology [8,31]. Because TTA is a statically scheduled architecture with high level of detail exposed to the programmer, the runtime efficiency of the end results produced with the design toolset depends heavily on the quality of the compiler. TCE uses the LLVM Compiler Infrastructure [13] as the backbone for its compiler tool chain (later referred to as 'tcecc'), thus benefits from its interprocedural optimizations such as aggressive dead code elimination and link time inlining. In addition to the target independent optimizations provided by the LLVM toolchain, the TCE code generator includes an instruction scheduler with TTA-specific optimizations, and a register allocator optimized to expose instruction-level parallelism to the post-pass scheduler. The register allocator is based on the LLVM implementation of the linear scan allocator [24] by adding round robin register assignment strategy to reduce the reuse of registers which hinders parallelism extraction.

3.2   TTA Vs. SPMD

A widespread programming model in GPUs is "Single Program, Multiple Data" (SPMD) [22]. In this model, the same code is executed on different computation units over different sets of data. This results in reduced instruction stream bandwidth usage. A straightforward implementation of this type of execution would be to replicate the control logic and datapath resources for every parallel running instance, essentially creating multiple simple independent processor cores that process their data independently from the others. To avoid this level of hardware complexity, a common solution [5] is to add groups of function units running on lockstep "Single Instruction, Multiple Data" (SIMD) mode, therefore sharing a common program counter and associated control logic by executing the same instruction on multiple compute units at the same time. In this type of setup, separate "SIMD groups" of function units may still be executing different parts of the program.

SIMD approach gives a good balance between hardware complexity and programming flexibility, but, in order to be efficient, the executed program must be data parallel, i.e. contain parts that can be efficiently vectorized. As the SIMD groups execute in lockstep, diverging branches where the number of parallel instances going into each branch is not a multiple of group size will cause hardware underutilization.

For an example, let us assume a SPMD machine with 8 groups of 32-way SIMD groups, therefore capable of running 256 instances ("threads") of a given program in parallel. Each thread is given a unique identifier (*thread_id*), so that the first 32 threads are run on the first SIMD group, the next 32 on the second group, and so on. In order to see the level of function unit idle time the "SIMD execution" can cause, let us consider a few example branching conditions:

(`thread_id % 2 == 0`) Every two consecutive threads take different branches. This causes half the function units on every SIMD group to be idle.

(`(thread_id >> 4) % 2 == 0`) Half the threads running on each group take different branches. Same utilization as above.

(`(thread_id >> 5) % 2 == 0`) Every thread in a group takes the same branch, thus no idle function units in this case. Perfect utilization.

(`thread_id < 215`) Only one of the groups has idle function units.

It has to be noted that this type of underutilization of function units does not result from compile-time unknown branching results, but from the intrinsic limitations on instruction scheduling capabilities of the SIMD-like microarchitecture. On the other hand, predicated TTA and VLIW programming models enable full utilization of function units for programs with compile-time known control flow.

As a result of the additional scheduling freedom and support for predicated execution, there are two clear cases where TTA/VLIW machines can outperform the throughput of SIMD machines with similar datapath resources (number of function units and register files).

1. Number of function units in the architecture does not match the number of "threads" in the program.
   If a program has less threads than computing elements in a SIMD group, TTA/VLIW processors allow using the extra computing resources to execute independent parts of the code within the threads itself. Consider a simple program structure like the following:

   ```
   A;
   if (P)
       B;
   C;
   ```

   where A, B and C are data-independent. This code is to be run in two parallel instances. Figure 3(a) shows how this example could be scheduled on a 3-way SIMD group. It can be clearly seen that one of the execution lanes is never used. Figure 3(b) shows how a predicated TTA/VLIW machine with the same number of function units can save a cycle out of three thanks to the scheduling freedom.

2. Runtime conditions allow "overcommitting" of datapath resources by means of predicated execution.

A TTA or VLIW architecture that supports overcommitting of resources allows scheduling two predicated operations to be executed in the same function unit at the same time instance, in case it is known at compile time that the predicates of the two operations are never simultaneously true [28]. Code suitable for overcommitting is often generated from *if...else* constructs. For example, consider the following program structure:

```
if (P)
    A;
else
    B;
C;
```

Suppose all operations are again independent, and two threads running on a 2-way group, Fig. 4(a) shows the resulting schedule for a SIMD machine: one third of the execution time is wasted for each lane. An overcommitting schedule for TTA, as shown in Fig. 4(b) saves that third cycle and results every computing element being used on each cycle. While it is possible to make an

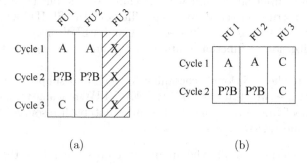

(a)   (b)

Fig. 3. Scheduling example showing TTA scheduling freedom. Schedule for (a) predicated 3-way SIMD, and (b) predicated TTA or VLIW.

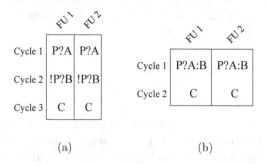

(a)   (b)

Fig. 4. Resource overcommitting example. Schedules for (a) predicated SIMD machine without overcommitting support, and (b) predicated TTA/VLIW with function unit overcommitting support. Question mark denotes predication of the succeeding statement with the preceding predicate, the possible negated statement is given after a colon.

operation-programmed VLIW to support overcommitting of resources, doing so requires double width instruction words that are otherwise unused most of the time. In case of TTA, in which instructions specify bus transports instead of operations, it is relatively common that some of the buses are unused on each cycle, thus overcommitting does not dramatically add to the instruction width penalty.

3.3   Scheduling a Real Shader

In order to study the practical advantages of TTA over SPMD, let us consider a shader taken from [25] that gives the rendered surfaces a wood-like appearance by using an externally (host-side) generated noise texture. The vertex shader is relatively simple and just prepares some data for later per-fragment computations. No conditional or loop code is present. The fragment shader, however, has some characteristics that make it adequate for showing how TTA/VLIW scheduling freedom improves performance under certain circumstances.

A streamlined version of the fragment shader code is given on Fig. 5. In the SPMD model, each of the lockstep SIMD function units will execute that code over a different fragment. This means that no vector operations are performed even when vector types are used in shader code. The "vectorization" happens by computing several fragments in parallel. In other words, each vector element

```
/* ... */

uniform sampler3D Noise;

/* ... */

void main(void)
{
    vec3 noisevec = vec3(texture(Noise, MCposition * NoiseScale) *
        Noisiness);

    /* ... */

    r = fract((MCposition.x + MCposition.z) * GrainScale + 0.5);
    noisevec[2] *= r;
    if (r < GrainThreshold)
        color += LightWood * LightGrains * noisevec[2];
    else
        color -= LightWood * DarkGrains * noisevec[2];

    color *= LightIntensity;
    FragColor = vec4(color, 1.0);
}
```

Fig. 5. Wood appearance fragment shader

belongs to a different fragment. This can be better described as several scalar threads being processed in parallel, and has led to the usage of the term "SIMT" (single-instruction multiple-thread) as a substitute of SIMD [20].

This approach is optimum when the number of vertices to be processed is an integer multiple of the number of SIMD function units. As explained in the previous section, in other cases TTA/VLIW machines can benefit from their capability to extract parallelism from within one thread. In this case, for example, the multiplication of the color vector by scalar can be parallelized easily. As TTAs are statically-scheduled, and (depending on the graphic pipeline implementation) the number of fragments to be processed might be only known at run-time, to really make a benefit of the scheduling freedom the compiler should generate several versions of the parallelized fragment shader, and choose the most suitable at run-time.

The other source of performance improvements come from the *if...else* construct in the code, in the very likely case that not every fragment being processed in parallel happens to run through the same conditional block. While one of the blocks is executed, SIMD units corresponding to fragments which have to go through the other block are going to be idle. The overcommitting capability of TTA/VLIW machines allows executing both blocks fully in parallel, avoiding this resource underutilization.

These two situations correspond to the cases where the TTA/VLIW scheduling freedom can provide performance benefits over the traditional SPMD execution model. Measurements of these improvements for the wood-appearance shader are given in the results section.

4   Software Graphics Pipeline

The TTAGPU OpenGL implementation is structured into two clearly separated parts. First part is the API layer, which is meant to be executed on the main CPU on the real scenario. It communicates with the GPU by a command queue, each command having a maximum of four floating-point arguments. Second part is the software implementation of the OpenGL graphics pipeline running in the TTA. We have tried to minimize the number of buffers to make the pipeline stages as long as possible, as this gives the compiler more parallelization opportunities.

The OpenGL graphics pipeline code includes both the software implementation of the pipeline routines itself, in addition to the user defined shader programs defined with GLSL. For the graphics pipeline code, we have so far implemented a limited version capable of doing simple rendering, allowing us to link against real OpenGL programs with no application code modification. Because tcecc already supports compilation of C and C++, it is possible to compile the user-defined GLSL code with a little additional effort by using C++ operator overloading and a simple preprocessor, and merge the shader code with the C implementation of the graphics pipeline.

Compiling GLSL code together with the C-based implementation of the graphics pipeline allows user-provided shaders to override the programmable parts, while providing an additional advantage of interprocedural optimizations and code specialization that is done after the final program linking. For example, if a custom shader program does not use a result produced by some of the fixed functionality of the graphics pipeline code, the pipeline code might get removed by the dead code elimination optimization. That is, certain types of fragment shader programs compiled with the pipeline code can lead to higher rasterizer performance.

Preliminary profiling of the current software graphics pipeline implementation showed that the bottleneck so far is on the rasterizer, and, depending on its complexity, on the user-defined fragment shader. This makes sense as the data density on the pipeline explodes after rasterizing, as usually a high number of fragments are generated by each primitive. Thus, in TTAGPU we concentrated on optimizing the rasterizer stage by creating a specialized rasterizer loop which processes 16 fragments at a time.

The combined rasterizer/custom fragment shader loop (pseudocode shown in Fig. 6) is fully unrolled by the compiler, implementing effectively a combined 16-way rasterizer and fragment processor on software. The aggressive procedure inlining converts the fully unrolled loop to a single big basic block with the actual rasterizer code producing a fragment and the user defined fragment shader processing it without the need for large buffers between the stages. In addition, the unrolled loop bodies are completely independent from each other, improving potential for high level of ILP exposed to the instruction scheduler. In order to avoid extra control flow in the loop which makes it harder to extract instruction level parallelism (ILP) statically, we always process 16 fragments at a time "speculatively" and discard the possible extra fragments at the end of computation.

```
for i = 1...16 do
    f = produce_fragment() // the rasterizer code
    f.invalid = i > number_of_fragments
    f = glsl_fragment_processor(f)
    if not f.invalid: write_to_framebuffer_fifo(f)
```

Fig. 6. Pseudocode of the combined rasterizer/fragment shader loop body.

If the primitive being rasterized generates a number of fragments that is not a multiple of 16 (a likely situation), some of the fragments will be marked as "invalid" and ignored during the framebuffer writing code. Although this means we are wasting resources in some cases, the improved degree of ILP greatly compensates for this when the number of fragments per primitive exceeds 16 by large, as it, according to our measurements, usually does.

5 Results

Two sets of results are presented. First, an evaluation of scalability of the TTAGPU using the software graphics pipeline implementation is performed. Second, in order to provide comparison with real commercial GPU hardware, we compare the performance of a TTAGPU against a GPU with SPMD execution model running the shader example presented in Sect. 3.

5.1 Instruction Level Scalability of the Graphics Pipeline

In order to assess the ILP scalability of the TTAGPU in the combined rasterizer/fragment processor loop, we implemented a simple example OpenGL application that renders lines randomly to the screen and colors them with a simple fragment shader. The goal of this experiment was to see how well the single TTAGPU cores scale at the instruction level only by adding different numbers of resource sets to the architecture and recompiling the software using tcecc. The resource set we used for scaling included a single FPU, three transport buses, and a register file with 32 general purpose 32 bit registers. The resources in the benchmarked TTAGPU variations are listed in Table 1.

Table 1. Resources of TTAGPUs used in experiments.

Resource	1 FPU	2 FPU	4 FPU	8 FPU	16 FPU
Floating point units	1	2	4	8	16
32 bit × 32 register files	1	2	4	8	16
1 bit Boolean registers	2	4	8	16	32
Transport buses	3	6	12	24	48
Integer ALUs	1	1	1	1	1
32 bit load-store units	1	1	1	1	1
32 bit shifters	1	1	1	1	1

The benchmark was executed using the TCE instruction cycle accurate processor architecture simulator for TTAGPUs with the different number of resource sets. Figure 7 shows the speedup improvements in the unrolled rasterizer loop caused by just adding multiples of the "scaling resource sets" to the machine and recompiling the code. This figure indicates that the ILP scalability of the heavily utilized rasterizer loop is almost linear thanks to the aggressive global optimizations and a register allocator that avoids the reuse of registers as much as possible, reducing the number of false dependencies limiting the parallelization between the loop iterations. The scaling gets worse when getting closer to the 16 FPU version because the loop was implemented with only 16 iterations. With a larger iteration count there would be more operations with which to hide the latencies of the previous iterations.

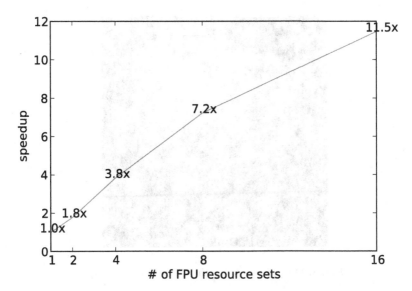

Fig. 7. Scalability of the rasterizer loop with different number of floating point resources.

5.2   Comparison Against a Real GPU

As our platform does not support the full OpenGL API so far, it is not easy to compare performance of a realistic rendering case. In order to produce some level of comparison, however, we have developed an OpenCL equivalent of the wood appearance fragment shader presented in Sect. 3.3. This allows us to abstract the rest of the pipeline, measuring the performance on this shader alone, taking its data from pre-generated buffers, on both our architecture and an nVidia GeForce 9400 graphic card. The OpenCL version follows closely the GLSL shader code and generates the colored pixels of the image. The resulting image is shown in Fig. 8.

As TTAGPU currently lacks vector load/store units, while nVidia cores can coalesce different buffer accesses into a single wide one, we have used different TTAGPU configurations with different number of load-store units (LSU). The 2-LSU case is realistically implementable on hardware, but as the resulting scheduled code is still slightly memory-access limited, we included results also for an 4-LSU version, as the performance is expected to be similar to this once the vector load/stores are added to the architecture. Aside from this, resources in the TTAGPU used for the measurements resemble those present in a single core of the GeForce card. The resources are summarized in Table 2.

Figure 9 presents cycle-count results for the execution of a single 32-wide work group. Numbers for NVIDIA were obtained using "Compute Visual Profiler" from their SDK, while TTAGPU was measured using the cycle-accurate simulator *ttasim* of TCE. The graph shows similar performance with 2-LSU TTAGPU and GeForce. TTAGPU is slightly faster when 4 LSUs are present, alleviating the

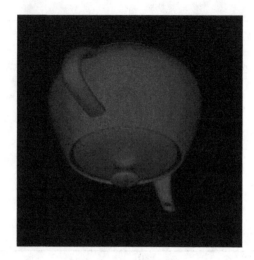

Fig. 8. Output image for the shader benchmark.

Table 2. Resources of the TTAGPUs used in the shader benchmark.

Resource	1 LSU	2 LSU	4 LSU
32 bit load-store units	1	2	4
Floating point units	8		
Extra floating point multipliers	8		
512×32 bit register files	8		
4×1 bit predicate register files	8		
Full integer ALUs	8		
Sqrt units	2		
Transport buses	48		

memory access bottleneck. Furthermore, when the execution causes the code to take diverging branches, it causes a cycle count penalty on nVidia case of about 11%, while it has no effect whatsoever on TTAGPU architecture due to the aggressive if-conversion and resource overcommitting.

In addition to reducing the effects of diverging branches to the throughput, the second case where TTAGPU is assumed to improve over SPMD is when the level of parallel execution does not perfectly match the function units of the core. In order to measure the effect from this, we executed the same benchmark with different work group sizes. Like expected, the cycle count does not change on the nVidia core when the number of work items is smaller than the available SIMD lanes, but on TTAGPU, the extra functional units can be used to speed up the execution. Figure 10 shows how the cycle count decreases with the size of the work group, with dashed lines marking the cycle count on the GeForce 9400. For work group sizes of 16 and below, half of the function units on the

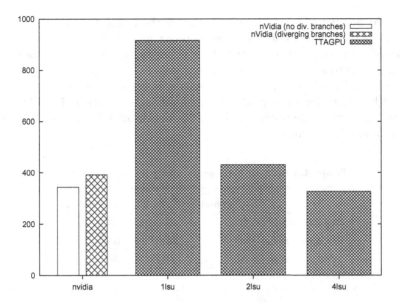

Fig. 9. Cycle counts for 32-wide workgroup execution.

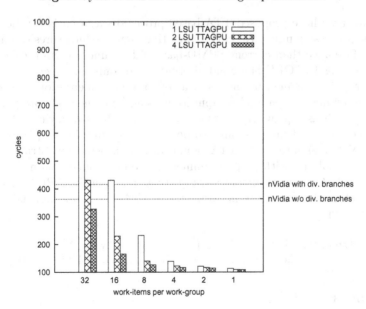

Fig. 10. Effect of the work group size on the cycle count for running the kernel.

nVidia core are idle, while the free scheduling of the resources allow TTAGPU to execute the kernel in much less cycles.

While overcommitting and scheduling freedom are provided by both TTA and VLIW, the latter suffers more from increased register file pressure when scaling the number of function units to match the instruction level parallelism available in the shader code. The unique programming model of TTA reduces this pressure by means of software register bypassing, often avoiding the need to save all results to general purpose registers already at compile time.

Results in Table 3 show about 34% decrease in register file accesses thanks to software bypassing for the OpenCL kernel under consideration. This significant reduction in register file traffic highlights the benefit of TTA over a VLIW with similar datapath resources.

Table 3. Effects of bypassing on register file pressure.

	No bypassing	Bypassing	Reduction
Register reads	4897	3304	33%
Register writes	3483	2258	35%
Total accesses	8380	5562	34%

6   Conclusions

In this paper we have proposed TTA-based processors as a basis for the design of graphic processing units. We have shown that these architectures can achieve better performance than current SPMD-based GPUs under certain conditions. In addition, the TTAGPU is a good alternative not only for executing the traditional graphics pipeline, by means of a software implementation, but also as a platform for massive parallel computation using heterogeneous programming languages (such as OpenCL) designed to run on GPU-like devices. Although most of the TTA's advantages can also be realized in traditional operation programmed VLIW architectures, TTA significantly improves the instruction level parallelism scalability with its programmer-visible interconnection network.

Future TTAGPU work includes completing the OpenGL API implementation, evaluating the multi-core performance of TTAGPU, and implementing an FPGA prototype.

Acknowledgments. This research was partially funded by the Academy of Finland, the Nokia Foundation, and Finnish Center for International Mobility (CIMO).

References

1. Colwell, R.P., Nix, R.P., O'Donnell, J.J., Papworth, D.B., Rodman, P.K.: A VLIW architecture for a trace scheduling compiler. In: Proceedings of 2nd International Conference on Architectural Support for Programming Languages and Operating Systems, pp. 180–192. IEEE Computer Society Press, Los Alamitos (1987). https://doi.org/10.1145/36206.36201
2. Corporaal, H.: Microprocessor Architectures: From VLIW to TTA. Wiley, Chichester (1997)

3. Corporaal, H.: TTAs: missing the ILP complexity wall. J. Syst. Arch.: EUROMICRO J. **45**(12–13), 949–973 (1999). https://doi.org/10.1016/S1383-7621(98)00046-0
4. Crow, T.S.: Evolution of the graphical processing unit. Master's thesis, University of Nevada, Reno (2004)
5. Fatahalian, K., Houston, M.: A closer look at GPUs. Commun. ACM **51**(10), 50–57 (2008)
6. Halfhill, T.R.: Parallel processing with CUDA. Microprocessor Report (2008)
7. Hoogerbrugge, J., Corporaal, H.: Register file port requirements of transport triggered architectures. In: Proceedings of 27th International Symposium on Microarchitecture, pp. 191–195. ACM, New York (1994). https://doi.org/10.1145/192724.192751
8. Jääskeläinen, P., Guzma, V., Cilio, A., Takala, J.: Codesign toolset for application-specific instruction-set processors. In: Proceedings of SPIE Multimedia on Mobile Devices 2007, vol. 6507 (2007)
9. Jääskeläinen, P., de La Lama, C.S., Huerta, P., Takala, J.: OpenCL-based design methodology for application-specific processors. In: 10th International Conference on Embedded Computer Systems: Architectures, Modeling and Simulation, July 2010, to appear
10. Kessenich, J.: The OpenGL Shading Language. 3DLabs, Inc. (2006)
11. Khronos Group: OpenCL 1.0 Specification (2009). http://www.khronos.org/registry/cl/
12. de La Lama, C.S., Jääskeläinen, P., Takala, J.: Programmable and scalable architecture for graphics processing units. In: Bertels, K., Dimopoulos, N., Silvano, C., Wong, S. (eds.) SAMOS 2009. LNCS, vol. 5657, pp. 2–11. Springer, Heidelberg (2009). https://doi.org/10.1007/978-3-642-03138-0_2
13. Lattner, C., Adve, V.: LLVM: a compilation framework for lifelong program analysis & transformation. In: Proceedings of International Symposium on Code Generation and Optimization: Feedback-Directed and Runtime Optimization. IEEE Computer Society, Washington (2004)
14. Lindholm, E., Nickolls, J., Oberman, S., Montrym, J.: NVIDIA Tesla: a unified graphics and computing architecture. IEEE Micro **28**(2), 39–55 (2008)
15. Lorie, R.A., Hovey R. Strong, J.: Method for conditional branch execution in SIMD vector processors. US Patent 4435758 (1984)
16. Luebke, D., Humphreys, G.: How GPUs work. Computer **40**(2), 96–100 (2007)
17. Moy, S., Lindholm, J.E.: Method and system for programmable pipelined graphics processing with branching instructions. US Patent 6947047 (2005)
18. Moya, V., González, C., Roca, J., Fernández, A., Espasa, R.: Shader performance analysis on a modern GPU architecture. In: Proceedings of 38th IEEE/ACM International Symposium on Microarchitecture, pp. 355–364 (2005)
19. Nickolls, J., Dally, W.: The GPU computing era. IEEE Micro **30**(2), 56–69 (2010). https://doi.org/10.1109/MM.2010.41
20. NVIDIA: CUDA programming guide v2.1. Technical report (2008)
21. NVIDIA: NVIDIA's next generation CUDA compute architecture: Fermi. White Paper (2009)
22. Owens, J.D., Houston, M., Luebke, D., Green, S., Stone, J.E., Phillips, J.C.: GPU computing. Proc. IEEE **96**(5), 879–899 (2008)
23. Owens, J.D., Luebke, D., Govindaraju, N., Harris, M., Krüger, J., Lefohn, A.E., Purcell, T.J.: A survey of general-purpose computation on graphics hardware. Comput. Graph. Forum **26**(1), 80–113 (2007)

24. Poletto, M., Sarkar, V.: Linear scan register allocation. ACM T. Program. Lang. Syst. **21**(5), 895–913 (1999). https://doi.org/10.1145/330249.330250
25. Rost, R.J.: OpenGL Shading Language, 3rd edn. Addison-Wesley, Reading (2010)
26. Segal, M., Akeley, K.: The OpenGL Graphics System: A Specification. Silicon Graphics, Inc. (2006)
27. Seiler, L., et al.: Larrabee: a many-core x86 architecture for visual computing. ACM Trans. Graph. **27**(3), 18 (2008)
28. Smelyanskiy, M., Mahlke, S.A., Davidson, E.S., Lee, H.H.S.: Predicate-aware scheduling: a technique for reducing resource constraints. In: Proceedings of International Symposium on Code Generation and Optimization: Feedback-Directed and Runtime Optimization. ACM International Conference Proceedings Series, vol. 37, pp. 169–178 (2003)
29. St-Laurent, S.: The Complete Effect and HLSL Guide. Paradoxal Press, Redmond (2005)
30. Stephens, R.: A survey of stream processing. Acta Inform. **34**(7), 491–541 (1997)
31. Tampere University of Technology: TCE project at TUT. http://tce.cs.tut.fi
32. Wasson, S.: AMD Radeon HD 2900 XT graphics processor: R600 revealed. Technical report (2007). http://www.techreport.com/reviews/2007q2/radeon-hd-2900xt/index.x?pg=1
33. Wasson, S.: NVIDIA's GeForce 8800 graphics processor. Technical report (2007). http://www.techreport.com/reviews/2006q4/geforce-8800/index.x?pg=1

Circular Buffers with Multiple Overlapping Windows for Cyclic Task Graphs

Tjerk Bijlsma[1]([✉]) [iD], Marco J. G. Bekooij[1,2], and Gerard J. M. Smit[1]

[1] University of Twente, 7500AE Enschede, The Netherlands
tjerk.bijlsma@gmail.com
[2] NXP Semiconductors Research, 5656AE Eindhoven, The Netherlands

Abstract. Multimedia applications process streams of values and can often be represented as task graphs. For performance reasons, these task graphs are executed on multiprocessor systems. Inter-task communication is performed via buffers, where the order in which values are written into a buffer can differ from the order in which they are read. Some existing approaches perform inter-task communication via first-in-first-out buffers in combination with reordering tasks and require applications with affine index-expressions. In our previous work, we used circular buffers with a non-overlapping read and write window, such that a reordering task is not required. However, these windows can cause deadlock for cyclic task graphs.

In this paper, we introduce circular buffers with multiple overlapping windows that do not delay the release of locations and therefore they do not introduce deadlock for cyclic task graphs. We show that buffers with multiple overlapping read and write windows are attractive, because they avoid that a buffer has to be selected from which a value has to be read or into which a value has to be written. This significantly simplifies the extraction of a task graph from a sequential application. These buffers are also attractive, because a buffer capacity equal to the array size is sufficient for deadlock-free execution, instead of performing global analysis to compute sufficient buffer capacities. Our case-study presents two applications that require these buffers.

Keywords: Multiple overlapping windows · Cyclic task graph ·
Sliding windows · Inter-task communication ·
Arbitrary index-expressions · Deadlock-free execution

1 Introduction

Multimedia applications are often executed on multiprocessor systems for performance reasons. These applications process streams of values and can be represented as task graphs. The tasks in these task graphs are executed in parallel and communicate values via buffers. A value can be read from a buffer after it

© Springer-Verlag GmbH Germany, part of Springer Nature 2019
P. Stenström et al. (Eds.): Transactions on HiPEAC V, LNCS 11225, pp. 39–58, 2019.
https://doi.org/10.1007/978-3-662-58834-5_3

has been written, otherwise the reading task has to be blocked until the value has been written, this requires synchronization between the tasks.

Parallelization tools for multiprocessor systems with a distributed memory architecture are presented in [11,12,14]. To pipeline the execution of an application, inter-task communication is performed via First-In-First-Out (FIFO) buffers. Therefore, if the write order of values in a FIFO buffer differs from the order in which the values have to be read, a reordering task has to reorder the values in a reordering buffer. This task becomes complex if it has to keep track of values that are read multiple times. To determine the behavior of the reordering task, affine index-expressions are required for the two communicating tasks, where an affine index-expression is limited to a summation of variables multiplied with constants plus an additional constant, e.g. $x[i_0 + 2i_1 + 4]$, with i_0 and i_1 the variables.

An other approach for inter-task communication between a reading and writing task is presented in [4]. A non-overlapping sliding Read Window (RW) and Write Window (WW) are used in a so called Circular Buffer (CB), as depicted in Fig. 1. The windows are called sliding, because a location is added to the head of the window before each access, and the location at the tail is released from the window after an access. Sliding windows will be discussed in detail in Sect. 5.1. The size of a window is computed such that during each access the location to be accessed is in the window. This approach is attractive, because the locations in a window can be accessed in an arbitrary order and an arbitrary number of times, without the need for a reordering task or reordering buffer. Because such a reordering task is not required, a broader class of applications can be supported, including applications with non-affine index-expressions.

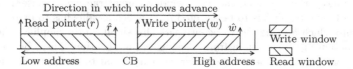

Fig. 1. Buffer with a sliding read and write window.

However, for a cyclic task graph the use of non-overlapping sliding windows can lead to deadlock, which we will demonstrate with the didactical example in Fig. 2(a). The tasks t_1 and t_2 communicate via the buffers s_x and s_y, according to the sequential code given beside the tasks. Task t_2 calls the non-affine function F, which is depicted in Fig. 2(b). The symbol $\sim$ depicts code that is omitted for clarity.

Figure 3 depicts the read and write patterns for the tasks in Fig. 2(a). The RW and WW in CB s_x and the RW in s_y have one location, because the locations are accessed in FIFO order. The WW in s_y requires four locations, due to the irregular access pattern computed by F. A location may not be released from this WW before it has been written. Therefore, the locations 1 and 2 in s_y are not released from the WW until location 0 has been written, as indicated in Fig. 3. In this figure, the delayed release of location 1 from the WW in s_y is depicted in bold and inside a gray box, because it causes deadlock. To release location 1 from its WW in s_y, task t_2 first has to write location 3 in s_y and read location 3 from s_x. Before t_1 writes location 3 in s_x and releases it from its WW, it has to read location 1 from s_y. As a consequence, there is a cyclic dependency between t_2 and t_1, where t_2 does not release location 1 from its WW in s_y, because t_1 does not release location 3 from its WW in s_x and vice versa. Because location 1 is not immediately released from the WW in CB s_y after it is written by t_2, the tasks deadlock.

s_x

t_1　　　s_y　　　t_2

```
int F(int j){
  if(j<2){
    return j+1;
  }else if (j ==2){
    return 0;
  }else{
    return j;
}}
```

```
x[0] = ~;
x[1] = ~;
for(int i=2;i≤5;i++){        for(int j=0;j≤5;j++){
  x[i] = y[i − 1];             y[F(j)] = x[j];
}                           }
```
(a)　　　　　　　　(b)

Fig. 2. (a) Task graph with a cyclic dependency between task t_1 and t_2 and (b) the non-affine function F called by task t_2.

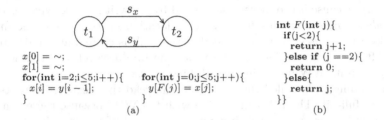

Fig. 3. Locations read and written by the tasks from Fig. 2.

Buffers with only one reading and one writing task can introduce problems during automatic parallelization, this is the so called *buffer selection problem*. For this problem, an array that is initially written by multiple assignment-statements is replaced by multiple FIFO buffers. Each of the writing tasks writes its own FIFO buffer, but the reading task needs a function to select per value from which FIFO buffer it has to be read. Extracting a simple function can be difficult, if the application contains non-affine index-expressions. We discuss the buffer selection problem in detail, in Sect. 4.

In this paper, we present a CB with multiple overlapping windows for the inter-task communication between multiple reading and writing tasks in cyclic task graphs with arbitrary index-expressions. Overlapping windows do not intro-duce deadlock for cyclic task graphs, because a location is released from the WW immediately after it is written. The support of multiple overlapping windows is an extension to the CB with overlapping windows presented in [3]. The main advantage of a buffer with multiple overlapping windows is that it avoids the buffer selection problem. A new insight is that a window with a size equal to the array size can hide non-affine and even data dependent access patterns. Furthermore, a buffer capacity equal to the array size is sufficient for deadlock-free execution, such that we do not need global analysis to compute sufficient buffer capacities.

A CB with overlapping windows cannot cause deadlock for cyclic task graphs, because a written location is released *immediately* from the WW. Therefore, each location in the CB has a *full-bit* that is set if the location contains a value. The novelty of our full-bit is that it does not require atomic read-modify-write operations, because it is only set and cleared by the writing task, which is called the *producer*. Before the producer writes a location in its window, the full-bit of the location consecutive to the head of the WW is cleared and added to the WW. After writing a value to a location, the producer releases this location directly from its WW by setting its full-bit.

The reading task, called the *consumer*, can read the locations from its RW with a set full-bit. The RW can overlap with the WW, because there can be a sequence of locations from which some can be read while other locations still have to be written. After reading a location in the RW, the consumer releases the location at the tail of its RW.

We generalize a CB with overlapping windows towards a CB with multiple overlapping WWs and RWs. This generalization is non trivial, because it requires per WW a full-bit per location in the CB.

In a CB with multiple WWs and RWs, the windows can advance independently of each other, thereby enabling the parallel and pipelined execution of the producers and consumers. Overlapping multiple RWs is possible, because a location in the CB can be read multiple times before it is removed from the RWs. Multiple WWs can overlap without causing race-conditions, because we require the task graph to contain Single Assignment (SA) code and therefore each location in a CB is written by at most one task.

The full-bit per location per WW forms also a cost for using multiple overlapping windows in a CB, compared to using non-overlapping sliding windows in a CB. An additional cost is the execution of the set and clear operation for the full-bits by the producer.

In our case-study we will examine two applications with cyclic task graphs. In the first task graph, the cycle is caused by the cyclic data dependency in a while-loop. The second application is a typical channel decoder, where the mode switching causes the cycle. Both task graphs contain a cycle and arrays that are accessed by multiple tasks. CBs with multiple overlapping windows enable the parallel execution of the tasks from these task graphs.

The organization of this paper is as follows. In Sect. 2, the related work is discussed. Subsequently, Sect. 3 presents the supported applications. For these applications, Sect. 4 addresses the buffer selection problem that occurs if multiple producers communicate with multiple consumers. As a solution to the buffer selection problem, we use CBs with multiple overlapping windows, as explained in Sect. 5. The intuition behind the insertion of synchronization and communication statements into the tasks to use these CBs is presented in Sect. 6. In the case study in Sect. 7, we examine two applications that require CBs with multiple overlapping windows. Finally, conclusions are drawn in Sect. 8.

2 Related Work

The Compaan approach [13] uses FIFO buffers for inter-task communication that have at most one producer and consumer. Initially, an array can be written by multiple tasks from a task graph. To insert FIFO buffers, each producer is transformed to write its own FIFO buffer and a condition is inserted in the Nested Loop Program (NLP) of the consumer, to determine per read access the FIFO to be read. Deriving such a condition is complex and requires affine index-expressions in the NLPs. In contrast, we use a CB with overlapping windows that can be written by multiple producers and read by multiple consumers, without requiring the derivation of a condition for a reading task.

The approach in [8] uses containers for inter-task communication, where a container is a place holder for values. Inside a container, locations can be accessed in any order and therefore a reordering task is not required. After values are written in a container the container is released such that the consumer can read from it. But, as for non-overlapping windows, a container is not accessible before it is completely filled with values and released, which may cause deadlock for cyclic task graphs. In a CB with overlapping windows, a written value is released immediately, such that it cannot introduce deadlock in cyclic task graphs.

The synchronization statements for our approach are not supported by current streaming libraries, as e.g. [15]. Their APIs only support that all locations in a window are either acquired for reading or writing, this results in non-overlapping windows. In contrast, our approach requires overlapping windows and therefore a synchronization statement that verifies that the location to be read contains a value, i.e. if its full-bit is set.

A full-empty bit for each location in an inter-task communication buffer is proposed in [6]. The producer sets the full-empty bit of a location after writing and the consumer clears the full-empty bit after reading a location for the last time. In contrast, we use full-bits that are only set or cleared by at most one producer when the location is added to or removed from the WW, respectively. Because only one producer sets and clears the full-bits, no atomic read-modify-write operations are required.

3 Input Applications

In this paper, an application is described by a task graph. Initially, these tasks communicate by reading from and writing in arrays. Such a task graph can be extracted from a sequential NLP by automatic parallelization, as for example presented in [13]. A task graph can be extracted from a sequential NLP with SA code, this means that for one execution of the sequential NLP a location in an array is written at most once. For a task graph, this results in a location in an array to be written by at most one task, if each task is executed once. We require a task graph with this property. Because a detailed discussion about automatic parallelization of a SA sequential NLP is outside the scope of this paper, we assume the resulting task graph as input to our approach.

A task graph is represented by a directed graph $H = \{T, S, A, \sigma, \theta\}$ that may contain cycles. The set of vertices is T. Each vertex $t_i \in T$ represents a task, where the functional behavior of a task is defined by an NLP. For a stream, a task is executed an infinite number of times. The set of arrays is A. Each array $a_j \in A$ is declared in an NLP. The set S represents the directed hyperedges. A hyperedge $s_j = (\{t_h \mid t_h \in T\}, \{t_i \mid t_i \in T\})$, with $s_j \in S$, is from the tasks in the set $\{t_h \mid t_h \in T\}$ to the tasks in the set $\{t_i \mid t_i \in T\}$. Each edge represents a buffer. In a buffer s_j the values of the corresponding array a_j are stored. The size, in number of locations, of the array a_j is given by $\sigma(a_j)$, with $\sigma : A \to \mathbb{N}$. The capacity of buffer s_j is the number of locations $\theta(s_j)$, with $\theta : S \to \mathbb{N}$.

For the accesses of tasks in arrays, three interesting access patterns are identified, i.e. out-of-order access, multiplicity, and skipping [3,8,12]. We define the *out-of-order* access pattern as the access of non-consecutive locations in an array. The *multiplicity* access pattern occurs if a location is accessed more than once. The *skipping* pattern occurs if a location is written in the array, but not read.

4   Inter-task Communication Between Multiple Producers and Consumers

Initially, NLPs read or write arrays. To execute a task graph on a multiprocessor system, these array accesses should be replaced by communication via one or more buffers. If multiple NLPs read or write an array, the array can be replaced by multiple FIFO buffers or a buffer that supports multiple producers and consumers. If multiple FIFO buffers have to be used, the *buffer selection problem* occurs. In this section, we will show that a buffer for multiple producers and consumers drastically simplifies the inter-task communication, because it avoids the buffer selection problem. Therefore, we will first discuss the buffer selection problem for the consumer that occurs if multiple tasks write into one array. Subsequently, the buffer selection problem for the producer is discussed that occurs if multiple tasks read from one array.

Figure 4 illustrates the buffer selection problem for the consumer. In Fig. 4(a), the tasks t_0 and t_1 write into array x and t_2 reads from x and the communication via array x should be replaced by communication via a buffer. In Fig. 4(b), the tasks t_0 and t_1 are merged into a single task, such that a buffer s_x that is suitable for only one producer and one consumer can be used. However, merging these tasks is undesirable, because it limits the amount of parallel execution in the task graph.

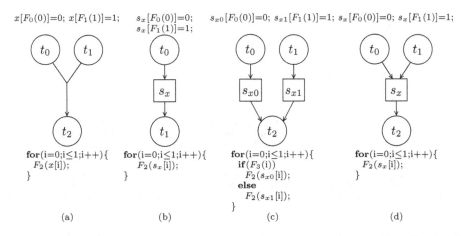

Fig. 4. (a) Task graph in which the communication via array x is replaced by (b) a single buffer s_x by merging the writing tasks, (c) two FIFO buffers s_{x0} and s_{x1} that are read by task t_2 using a condition, or alternatively (d) a buffer s_x that supports multiple writing tasks.

Figure 4(c) and (d) illustrate two approaches that replace the communication via an array by communication via a buffer, without limiting the parallel execution of the tasks. Figure 4(c) depicts the first approach, where each writing task writes into its own FIFO buffer. This requires an if-condition with a function F_3 in the reading task t_2 that selects from which buffer a value has to be read. This is what we call the *buffer selection problem for the consumer*. The approach in [13] requires affine index-expressions to derive a simple function for the consumer. In Fig. 4(c), t_0 and t_1 have non-affine index-expressions, due to the called functions F_0 and F_1 and therefore no simple function F_3 can be derived for t_2.

An alternative to using FIFO buffers is a buffer that can be written by multiple tasks, as depicted in Fig. 4(d). Such a buffer does not require the derivation of a function that selects the buffer to be read and therefore simplifies the inter-task communication.

Figure 5 illustrates the buffer selection problem for the producer. In Fig. 5(a), t_0 writes into array x that is read by the tasks t_1 and t_2. Figure 5(b) depicts the application of the two FIFO buffers s_{x0} and s_{x1}, for the inter-task communication. Because a value that is written into a FIFO buffer should also be read from it, t_0 should only write values into s_{x0} or s_{x1} that will be read by t_1 or t_2, respectively. Therefore, t_0 requires the functions F_4 and F_5 that select per FIFO buffer if a value has to be written into the FIFO buffer. This is what we call the *buffer selection problem for the producer*. The approach in [13] also requires affine index-expressions to derive a simple function that solves this problem. In Fig. 5(b), extracting a simple function can be difficult, due to the non-affine index-expressions of t_1 and t_2.

The alternative of writing into two different FIFO buffers is a buffer that can be read by multiple tasks, as depicted in Fig. 5(c). This buffer does not require

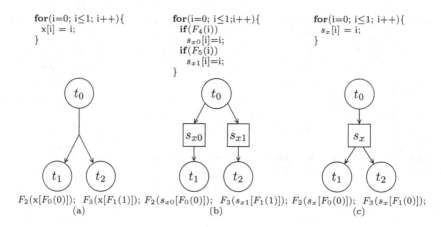

$F_2(x[F_0(0)]);$ $F_3(x[F_1(1)]);$ $F_2(s_{x0}[F_0(0)]);$ $F_3(s_{x1}[F_1(1)]);$ $F_2(s_x[F_0(0)]);$ $F_3(s_x[F_1(0)]);$
(a)   (b)   (c)

Fig. 5. (a) Task graph in which the communication via array x is replaced by (b) two FIFO buffers s_{x0} and s_{x1} that are written by t_0 using a condition or alternatively (c) a buffer s_x that supports multiple reading tasks.

a function to be derived for the producer and therefore simplifies the inter-task communication.

Figures 4(d) and 5(c) show how a buffer that supports *multiple producers and multiple consumers* drastically simplifies the inter-task communication, as no functions have to be derived. Therefore, we will introduce such a buffer in the next section.

5   Multiple Overlapping Windows in a Circular Buffer

In this section, we present inter-task communication via a CB with read and write windows. In a CB, a task has a window that contains a number of locations that it can read or write in an arbitrary order and read multiple times. This window can hide any access pattern and therefore no reordering task is required. Furthermore, each task only updates its own part of the buffer administration, such that we do not require atomic read-modify-write operations. The tasks can advance their windows independently of each other in the CB and therefore the parallel and pipelined execution of the producer and consumer is possible.

In Sect. 5.1, we start by explaining a CB with a non-overlapping RW and WW that do not cause deadlock in acyclic task graphs. Subsequently, Sect. 5.2 extends these non-overlapping windows in a CB to an overlapping RW and WW that do not introduce deadlock for cyclic task graphs. In Sect. 5.3, CBs with overlapping windows are generalized to contain multiple overlapping RWs and WWs, such that we avoid the buffer selection problem.

5.1   A Circular Buffer with a Sliding Read and Write Window

This section explains a CB with a non-overlapping sliding RW and WW that can be applied for acyclic task graphs. These windows hide the irregular access pattern of their task and result in regular synchronization. The buffer administration for sliding windows contains a pointer to the head and the tail for each window.

The tasks that communicate by reading from and writing into a buffer are executed in parallel, possibly on different processors. A value may only be read after it has been written and therefore the reading task should be blocked if it attempts to read an unwritten location. Blocking is necessary, because our processors do not run in lockstep, as is assumed in [10]. For a system running in lockstep, the processors synchronize the execution of each operation, such that a global static schedule of operations can be computed, in which a value is never read before it is written. Our processors execute in parallel. Therefore, the order in which read and write operations in a buffer become visible and accessible for other processors is defined by a memory consistency model. We rely on the memory consistency models in [5, 7], because we perform synchronization using acquire and release calls. Before accessing a location we perform an *acquire* call for it, this function blocks until the location is signaled to be available. Succeeding the access to a location a *release* call signals that the location is available. A location acquired for writing cannot be acquired by the consumer for reading before the producer released it.

We use a CB for the inter-task communication. A CB can be implemented with a read pointer r and a write pointer w, as depicted in Fig. 1. The locations between r and w in the CB can be read in an arbitrary order, thereby supporting the multiplicity, skipping, and out-of-order access patterns that have been explained in Sect. 3. Between w and r in the CB, arbitrary locations can be written. The pointer w or r can be incremented, to make a location available for reading or writing, respectively. A pointer that reaches the end of the CB is wrapped around to the beginning of the CB.

In a CB, starting at r a number of consecutive locations are acquired that form a RW, where $\hat{r}$ points to the location at the head of this window. Similarly, starting at w a number of consecutive acquired locations form a WW, with $\hat{w}$ pointing to the head of the window. For a window the pointer to its head and the pointer to its tail administrate the consecutive acquired locations. Both tasks have random access in their window.

For the inter-task communication via a CB, the reading or writing of an array element k will be changed into the reading or writing of the corresponding location k in a CB.

Inter-task communication is performed via a CB with a *non-overlapping* RW and WW, in [4]. Preceding an access to a location in the window, a task acquires the location consecutive to the head of the window by incrementing the pointer to the head of the window. Succeeding an access, the location at the tail of the window is released by incrementing the pointer to the tail of the window. As for r and w, also $\hat{r}$ and $\hat{w}$ wrap around if they reach the end of the CB. This results in a sliding RW and WW, as depicted in Fig. 1.

The regular synchronization pattern for a window hides the irregular access pattern of its task inside the window, such that we do not require a potentially complex reordering task. Furthermore, atomic read-modify-write operations are not required in the multiprocessor system, because the producer only updates w and $\hat{w}$ and the consumer r and $\hat{r}$.

The main limitation of non-overlapping windows is that they can introduce deadlock in a cyclic task graph, because the location written in the WW is not necessarily the location that is released. The delayed release of a location from the WW and the cyclic dependencies can cause deadlock, as illustrated in the example in the introduction.

5.2   A Circular Buffer with an Overlapping Read and Write Window

In this section, we extend sliding windows towards overlapping windows, such that we do not introduce deadlock for cyclic task graphs. We avoid deadlock, by using a full-bit per location that is set immediately after the location is written, such that the location can be read. As sliding windows, overlapping windows do not require atomic read-modify-write operations. In addition, they can hide any access pattern.

For cyclic dependencies, as illustrated in Fig. 2, a value should be available for reading directly after it has been written. This requires the producer to release a written location directly from its WW, such that the consumer can acquire it for reading. In contrast, the location at w is released from a non-overlapping WW after writing at location k, where w does not necessary equal k. To avoid deadlock, it has to be possible to read the written location k that is possibly after location w, i.e. between w and $\hat{w}$. Therefore, we have to allow reading between w and $\hat{w}$ in the CB, which results in an *overlapping* RW and WW, as depicted in Fig. 6.

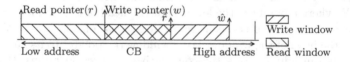

Fig. 6. CB with an overlapping RW and WW.

For overlapping windows, per location in the WW it should be administrated if it can be acquired for reading. This can be done with a *full-bit* that is cleared when its location is acquired for writing and set directly after a value is written at its location. A location in the RW with a set full-bit can be acquired for reading.

A full-bit can either be stored along with its location or in the buffer administration. Some architectures [1,2] provide an additional bit for every location in the shared memory that can be used as a full-bit. An alternative is to store full-bits in the buffer administration by using a bit vector, with a full-bit for each location in the CB.

Before writing a location, the producer acquires a location for its WW. To acquire a location for its WW, the producer clears the full-bit of the location consecutive to $\hat{w}$ and acquires this location by incrementing $\hat{w}$. Note that $\hat{w}$ cannot overtake r. Therefore, if r is the location consecutive to $\hat{w}$, the clearing of the full-bit and the acquire are blocked until r is incremented. After writing a location, it is released from the WW by setting the full-bit of this location. Note that for locations in the buffer that are not written, the full-bit will not be set, because these locations will also not be read.

To read a location in a CB the consumer acquires this location. The acquire call for a location checks if the full-bit of the location is set and that the location is not after $\hat{w}$, otherwise the acquire operation blocks. After reading a location, the consumer releases the location at r by incrementing it.

Updating the read pointer r, $\hat{w}$, and full-bits requires no atomic read-modify-write operations, as for example test-and-set and fetch-and-add. These operations are not required, because r is only updated by the consumer and $\hat{w}$ and the full-bits only by the producer. Note that due to the full-bits, overlapping windows do not need $\hat{r}$ and w.

Replacement of the communication via arrays in an NLP by CBs in a task graph will not introduce deadlock, if the CBs have overlapping windows and a capacity of at least the size of the arrays. The reason is that, by definition, the sequential NLP from which our task graph is extracted cannot deadlock, because it does not contain synchronization statements. From the fact that the sequential execution of the NLP is deadlock-free, we can conclude that there exists a sequential schedule that defines an order in which we can execute the assignment-statements in the NLP. After replacing the arrays by CBs with overlapping windows, in which the CBs have a capacity of at least the size of the arrays, and replacing the assignment-statements in the NLP by tasks in a task graph, we can conclude that these tasks can be executed in the same order. The reason is that values written in these CBs are directly available for reading. Allowing other execution orders of the tasks is equivalent to the removal of the sequence constraints that enforce the sequential schedule of the tasks. Furthermore, it is known that the task graph is functionally deterministic, because the firing rules of the tasks are sequential [9]. Removal of sequence constraints from a schedule of a functional deterministic task graph cannot introduce additional cyclic dependencies and therefore cannot introduce deadlock. Because there exists a schedule of the tasks in the task graph and removal of the constraints that enforce this schedule cannot result in deadlock, we conclude that the extracted task graph with overlapping windows is always deadlock-free.

An nice element of the overlapping windows in a CB s_x is that they can support *any* access pattern, including the access patterns of parameterized and data dependent index-expressions, if the RW and the WW are as large as the array size $\sigma(x)$. Inside an overlapping window, locations can be accessed in an arbitrary order and therefore no complex reordering task is required. If the access pattern in the buffer is known it is possible to compute smaller windows sizes and a smaller buffer capacity that also will not introduce deadlock.

5.3   A Circular Buffer with Multiple Overlapping Windows

In this section, we will generalize a CB with an overlapping RW and WW to contain multiple RWs and WWs, such that we avoid the buffer selection problems. As for overlapping windows, multiple overlapping windows do not require atomic read-modify-write operations and can support any access pattern.

Figure 7 depicts a CB with *multiple overlapping RWs and WWs*. Each consumer has a RW_n with an r_n. Multiple RWs can overlap, because a location can be read multiple times among different consumers. Each producer has a WW_n with a $\hat{w}_n$. The WWs of the producers can overlap, because at most one producer will write at a location in the buffer.

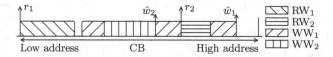

Fig. 7. A CB with four overlapping windows, two RWs and two WWs.

For multiple overlapping windows we do not want to depend upon atomic read-modify-write operations like test-and-set and fetch-and-add, because using such operations requires support from the underlying multiprocessor system. Without such operations, a value in the buffer administration can be written and read at the same moment, this results in fair access for the tasks, without unnecessary blocking.

If there are multiple producers in a CB with overlapping windows and only one full-bit per location, the first producer to acquire a location for its WW has to clear the full-bit of this location. If multiple producers can acquire such a location simultaneously, each of them will clear the full-bit of this location, where the clear operation of one of these producers can be delayed. This clear operation could be delayed that much, such that it is executed after an other producer has written the location and set its full-bit. Such a delayed clear operation may cause a race-condition and should therefore be avoided by using an atomic read-modify-write operation for the acquire call. We avoid race-conditions, without depending on atomic read-modify-write operations, by providing each producer its own full-bit for each location in the CB. In this case, there is at most one producer that writes to a full-bit.

For multiple overlapping RWs and WWs, the acquire and release operations for the producer and the consumer and the write operation are slightly changed. For a read pointer r_m and a $\hat{w}_n$, we store the location in the buffer to which they are pointing. For r_m and $\hat{w}_n$, we also store a *wrap counter* r_m^c and $\hat{w}_n^c$ that is increased every time its pointer wraps around in the buffer and is stored modulo 3. We need a wrap counter, because in a buffer with multiple WWs, a RW can (partly) overtake a WW and this WW should be allowed to overtake the RW again. An acquire operation for a WW_n for which r_m is the location consecutive to $\hat{w}_n$ does not block if the wrap counters are equal, because in this case WW_n runs behind the RW_m. If they have unequal wrap counters, WW_n has wrapped around and its acquire for WW_n blocks, because the location consecutive to $\hat{w}_n$ is not yet released from RW_m. We change the write operation, such that it does not write a value into the buffer if the location to be written is before all read pointers, because this value will never be read anyway.

We change the acquire operation for a producer t in its WW_n. The acquire operation clears its own full-bit f_n that is consecutive to the location to which $\hat{w}_n$ points in the CB, i.e. the full-bit at location $\hat{w}_n + 1$, followed by increasing $\hat{w}_n$, only if the acquire operation is not blocked. The acquire operation for WW_n is blocked, if there is a consumer t_m with a read pointer r_m that is equal to $(\hat{w}_n + 1) \bmod \theta(s_x)$ and an unequal wrap counter $((r_m^c + 1) \bmod 3 = \hat{w}_n^c)$, or if there is a producer t_p with a $\hat{w}_l$ equal to $(\hat{w}_n + 1) \bmod \theta(s_x)$ and with an unequal wrap counter $((\hat{w}_l^c + 1) \bmod 3 = \hat{w}_n^c)$. The release operation of a producer t_n for a location k sets the full-bit f_n that the producer has for the location, i.e. the full-bit f_n at location $k \bmod \theta(s_x)$.

For a consumer, the acquire operation for a location is extended to check if one of the producers has written the location. A consumer can acquire location k, if there is a producer t_n that has the full-bit f_n for this location set and has the location in its WW_n. Otherwise, the acquire operation blocks. The release operation for a consumer t_n remains unchanged and increases r_n.

Because each producer has its own full-bit per location in the CB, no atomic read-modify-write operations are required for multiple overlapping windows. A tail r_n of a RW_n is only updated by the consumer that reads from RW_n. The head $\hat{w}_n$ of a WW_n is only updated by the producer that uses this WW for writing, and each producer sets and clears its own full-bits.

6   Insertion of Communication and Synchronization Statements

To execute the tasks of a task graph in parallel in a multiprocessor system, synchronization statements have to be inserted into the NLPs of the tasks and array communication has to be replaced by inter-task communication via multiple overlapping windows. This section sketches the replacement of array communication by read and write calls for a CB and the insertion of acquire and release statements into the NLPs, such that overlapping windows can be used by the applications in Sect. 7. The presented approach is compact and focused at the insertion of synchronization statements for an assignment-statement that reads from and writes into a CB. A detailed explanation of the insertion of appropriate synchronization statements can be found in [3].

Figure 8 depicts a synthetic task graph that we will use to illustrate the insertion of inter-task communication and synchronization statements. In this task graph, task t_2 and t_3 read from array a using the non-affine function F. Each value that is read from array a is used as argument for the function F_2 or F_3, but not for both functions. The task graph contains a cycle via the arrays

a and b, where array a contains 9 elements and array b 10 elements. Note that array b is written by both t_2 and t_3, but that they write different locations. The symbol $\sim$ denotes a code fragment that is omitted for clarity.

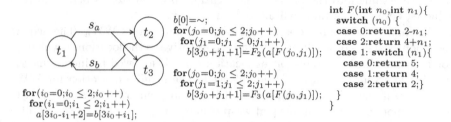

Fig. 8. Cyclic task graph with its NLPs and a non-affine function F called by t_2 and t_3.

For a task that uses a WW or a RW in a CB, a WW should contain the location to be written for each write access and a RW should contain the location to be read for each read access. Therefore, a write operation of a producer in its WW is preceded by acquiring a location for its WW. To make sure that the location to be written is acquired for each write operation, a producer may need to acquire a number of locations before its first write. This is what we call the *lead-in* for a producer. A consumer should not succeed each read operation with a release, to make sure that a location is not released before it has been read for the last time. The number of initial read accesses that are not succeeded by a release operation is called the *lead-out* for the consumer. Details about the computation of the lead-in and lead-out can be found in [3].

An alternative to computing the lead-in and lead-out for s_x is setting the lead-in equal to the array size ($\sigma(x)$) and the lead-out equal to the number of accesses in the array, thereby we enable the support of access patterns due to parametrized or data dependent index-expressions or arbitrary if-conditions. In this case, the lead-in acquires the whole array in advance, such that it can be written with an arbitrary pattern and the lead-out delays the releasing of locations from the RW until all read accesses have been performed. This results in a buffer capacity that is equal to the array size.

For a known access pattern we can typically compute a lead-in and lead-out, such that we can use windows that are smaller than the array size. By using these smaller windows in a CB with a buffer capacity equal to the size of the array, the executions of the communicating tasks can be pipelined. The execution can be pipelined, because producers can acquire locations for their WW for their next execution, while consumers still have locations for their current execution acquired.

We identify three phases, for an NLP with inserted synchronization statements, i.e. the initial phase, the processing phase, and the final phase, these are depicted in Fig. 9. The *initial phase* contains synchronization statements to acquire the lead-in for the CBs in which this NLP is going to write. The *processing phase* of an NLP contains the for-loops and assignment-statements. In this phase, the array accesses have been replaced by read and write statements for CBs and synchronization statements for these CBs encapsulate them. The *final phase* releases the remaining locations in the read CBs, due to the lead-out in the read CB.

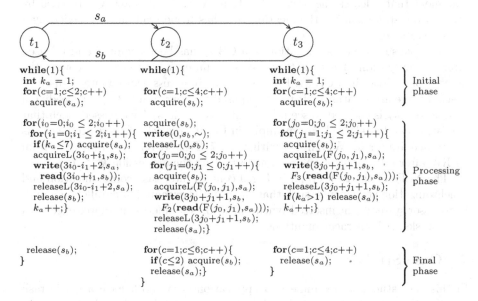

Fig. 9. Task graph from Fig. 8 with synchronization and communication statements inserted into the NLPs.

For the tasks in Fig. 8, t_1 has a lead-in of 1 location for CB s_a and t_2 and t_3 have a lead-in of 4 locations in s_b. These lead-ins are reflected in the number of acquired locations for the corresponding buffer, during the initial phases of the tasks in Fig. 9. The lead-out of t_1 in s_b is 0, the lead-out of t_2 in s_a is -2 and t_3 has a lead-out of 1 in s_a.

In Fig. 9, the array accesses of the NLPs in Fig. 8 have been replaced by read and write statements for CBs. In an assignment-statement, the write access to array a at location l_w is replaced by **write**(l_w, s_a, x), where s_a is the CB corresponding to array a and x the value to be written. The part of an assignment-statement that reads location l_r from array b is replaced with **read**(l_r, s_b), to read location l_r from CB s_b.

Two different acquire statements and release statements are required, for overlapping windows. The statement to acquire (release) the location consecutive to the head (tail) of the WW (RW) in s is *acquire(s)* (*release(s)*). In contrast, the statement to acquire (release) a location l with a value for the RW (WW) in s is $acquireL(l, s)$ $(releaseL(l, s))$. Both acquire statements are blocking, this means that they do not return until they succeed.

In the NLPs in Fig. 9, the assignment-statements are encapsulated by acquire and release statements for the read and written CBs. For a WW and a RW, the used acquire and release statements are asymmetric, such that locations can be acquired and released in the overlapping part of the RWs and WWs. A write call is preceded by an *acquire* statement and immediately succeeded by a *releaseL* statement that releases the written location. A read call is always preceded by an *acquireL* statement for the location that has to be read and succeeded by a *release* statement.

To make sure that each location in a CB s_x has been acquired and released after one execution of a task t, an access counter k_x is used that counts the number of accesses in a CB s_x. Preceding a write access, this counter is used to check if there are locations left to be acquired for a written CB s_x. Succeeding a read access, k_x is checked to see if lead-out accesses in s_x have passed, such that a location can be released. For example, in Fig. 9, t_1 checks if there are locations left to acquire for its WW in s_a, with $k_a \leq 7$. Task t_3 releases a location from its RW after a lead-out of one read access, using the expression $k_a > 1$.

The NLPs of the task graph in Fig. 9 contain inter-task communication and synchronization statements, such that they can be executed in parallel on a multiprocessor system. The inserted synchronization statements guarantee execution of the tasks without race-conditions.

7   Case Study

In this case study, we examine two applications that both have a cyclic task graph with arrays that are read and written by multiple tasks. The first application is the task graph of a while-loop, in which the expression of the condition depends upon a value written in the body of the for-loop, which causes the cycle in the task graph. The second application is a channel decoder that has to perform mode switching between decoding and detecting, where the reading and writing of the state causes a cycle in the task graph. Insertion of inter-task communication into these tasks is drastically simplified, by applying a CB with multiple overlapping windows.

An application with a *while-loop* is depicted in Fig. 10. Its task graph is partitioned over three tasks. Task t_c computes the condition, where the expression of the condition depends upon values read from array b that is written by t_1. Because each task requires the computed result of the condition and the computation of the result depends upon a value read from array b, the task graph is cyclic. Therefore, a buffer that supports cyclic data dependencies is essential. Furthermore non-affine index-expressions have to be supported, because t_c reads from array b using function F. Each array contains 100 elements, thus $\sigma(a) = \sigma(b) = \sigma(c) = \sigma(t) = 100$. Note that i and v are private variables that are not shared among the tasks and therefore not required to be SA.

Figure 11 depicts the tasks from Fig. 10 with communication and synchronization statements inserted, such that multiple overlapping windows are used for

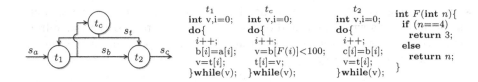

```
        t₁                    t_c                    t₂               int F(int n){
   int v,i=0;           int v,i=0;             int v,i=0;               if (n==4)
   do{                  do{                    do{                        return 3;
     i++;                 i++;                   i++;                  else
     b[i]=a[i];           v=b[F(i)]<100;         c[i]=b[i];             return n;
     v=t[i];              t[i]=v;                v=t[i];             }
   }while(v);          }while(v);             }while(v);
```

Fig. 10. Task graph of a data dependent while-loop.

the inter-task communication. Because the number of iterations of the while-loop is data dependent, the accesses in the array could not be derived by executing each task once. Instead, we assume that the locations can be accessed in any order and therefore for a CB all location are acquired during the initial phase and released during the final phase. The *acquireL* and *releaseL* operations have to be performed in the body of the while-loop, to release a location immediately after it is written.

```
        t₁                         t_c                          t₂
  while(1){                  while(1){                    while(1){
    int j,v,i=0;               int j,v,i=0;                 int j,v,i=0;
    for(j=0;j<100;j++)         for(j=0;j<100;j++)           for(j=0;j<100;j++)
      acquire(s_b);              acquire(s_t);                acquire(s_c);
    do{                        do{                          do{
      i++;                       i++;                         i++;
      acquireL(s_a,i);           acquireL(s_b,i);             acquireL(s_b,i);
      write(s_b,i,read(s_a,i));  v=read(s_b,F(i))<100;        write(s_c,i,read(s_b,i));
      releaseL(s_b,i);           write(s_t,i,v);              releaseL(s_c,i);
      acquireL(s_t,i);           releaseL(s_t,i);             acquireL(s_t,i);
      v=read(s_t,i);           }while(v);                     v=read(s_t,i);
    }while(v);                 for(j=0;j<100;j++)           }while(v);
    for(j=0;j<100;j++){          release(s_b);              for(j=0;j<100;j++){
      release(s_a);            }                              release(s_b);
      release(s_t);                                           release(s_t);
  }}                                                       }}
```

Fig. 11. Synchronization and communication statements inserted into the NLPs from Fig. 10.

The insertion of CBs with multiple overlapping windows into the tasks of Fig. 10 is straight forward. Because correct synchronization and communication statements are inserted, the NLPs in Fig. 11 can be executed in parallel. In contrast, to insert FIFO buffers for the inter-task communication, the buffer selection problem has to be solved, which may be difficult due to the non-affine index-expression of t_c in array b and the data dependent while-loop.

The task graph of a typical channel decoder is depicted in Fig. 12. The first task t_F contains the radio front-end that reads from s_a and writes samples in s_b. CB s_b is read by task t_{Det} that tries to *detect* a frame among the samples it reads from s_b. If t_{Det} detects a frame it notifies task t_{Dec} via s_c that it can *decode* frames from s_b and stops detecting. Task t_{Dec} keeps receiving frames until it reads an incorrect frame from s_b, after which it notifies t_{Det} via s_c and stops decoding. Due to the communication between t_{Det} and t_{Dec} via s_c, only one of these tasks writes in s_c and only one of the tasks processes a frame from s_b. Furthermore, the status in s_c determines if task t_P performs *processing* on the frames it reads from s_d.

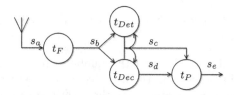

Fig. 12. Task graph of a channel decoder.

A channel decoder, as depicted in Fig. 12, contains cyclic dependencies via s_c and buffers that should be written and read by multiple tasks. In the task graph, frames are either detected by t_{Det} or decoded by t_{Dec}. Therefore, these tasks have to synchronize and communicate with each other, where both tasks can write data in buffer s_c. The multiple overlapping windows in a CB as we presented in this paper fit perfectly with this buffer, because t_{Det} and t_{Dec} can use it as a kind of shared memory by both having their own WW and RW in the CB. Because in this buffer the windows can overlap, the release of written values is not delayed, and therefore deadlock is not introduced.

8   Conclusion

In this paper, a circular buffer with multiple overlapping read and write windows is introduced that cannot cause deadlock in cyclic task graphs with arbitrary index-expressions. These buffers cannot cause deadlock for cyclic task graphs, because a written location is released immediately from a write window. Furthermore, the use of these buffers simplifies the insertion of inter-task communication statements by avoiding the buffer selection problem. These buffers are also attractive, because a buffer capacity equal to the array size is sufficient for deadlock-free execution, instead of performing global analysis to compute sufficient buffer capacities.

The windows used in the buffers by the tasks hide a possibly irregular access pattern of a task, with the regular synchronization pattern for the window. Therefore, no reordering tasks are required. Furthermore, if the size of a window is equal to the array size, it can hide any access pattern, even an access pattern due to a data dependent index-expression. The tasks can advance their windows independently of each other in a buffer, thereby enabling the parallel and pipelined execution of the producers and the consumers. Because each task only updates its own part of the buffer administration, we do not require support for atomic read-modify-write operations from the multiprocessor system.

In our case-study, we examined the cyclic task graph of a while-loop and of a typical channel decoder. Both applications contain a cycle and require buffers that support multiple reading and writing tasks. Circular buffers with multiple overlapping windows avoid deadlock for the inter-task communication in these applications.

The presented circular buffers with multiple overlapping windows enable inter-task communication for a broad class of applications that even includes cyclic task graphs with data dependent index-expressions. Interesting future work is an automatic parallelization approach that applies buffers with overlapping windows or sliding windows, which have a lower synchronization overhead, depending upon the extracted task graphs.

References

1. Agarwal, A., et al.: The MIT Alewife machine: architecture and performance. In: Proceedings of the International Symposium on Computer Architecture (ISCA), pp. 2–13. ACM, New York (1995)
2. Alverson, R., et al.: The Tera computer system. In: International Conference on Supercomputing (ICS), pp. 1–6. ACM, New York (1990)
3. Bijlsma, T., Bekooij, M.J.G., Smit, G.J.M.: Inter-task communication via overlapping read and write windows for deadlock-free execution of cyclic task graphs. In: Proceedings of the International Workshop on Systems, Architectures, Modeling, and Simulation (SAMOS), pp. 140–148. IEEE Computer Society, Los Alamitos, July 2009
4. Bijlsma, T., et al.: Communication between nested loop programs via circular buffers in an embedded multiprocessor system. In: Proceedings of the International Workshop on Software and Compilers for Embedded Systems (SCOPES), pp. 33–42. ACM, New York (2008)
5. van den Brand, J.W., Bekooij, M.J.G.: Streaming consistency: a model for efficient MPSoC design. In: Proceedings of the Euromicro Symposium on Digital System Design (DSD), pp. 27–34. IEEE Computer Society, Washington (2007)
6. Culler, D.E., Gupta, A., Singh, J.P.: Parallel Computer Architecture: A Hardware/Software Approach. Morgan Kaufmann, San Francisco (1999)
7. Gharachorloo, K., et al.: Memory consistency and event ordering in scalable shared-memory multiprocessors. In: Proceedings of the International Symposium on Computer Architecture (ISCA), pp. 15–26. ACM, New York (1990)
8. Huang, K., Grünert, D., Thiele, L.: Windowed FIFOs for FPGA-based multiprocessor systems. In: Proceedings of the International Conference on Application-Specific Systems, Architectures, and Processors (ASAP), pp. 36–42. IEEE Computer Society, Los Alamitos (2007)
9. Lee, E.A., Parks, T.M.: Dataflow process networks. Proc. IEEE 83(5), 773–801 (1995)
10. Oh, J., et al.: Exploiting thread-level parallelism in lockstep execution by partially duplicating a single pipeline. Electron. Telecommun. Res. Inst. (ETRI) J. 30(4), 576–586 (2008)
11. Turjan, A., Kienhuis, B., Deprettere, E.F.: Realizations of the extended linearization model in the Compaan tool chain. In: Proceedings of the International Workshop on Systems, Architectures, Modeling, and Simulation (SAMOS), pp. 1–24 (2002)

12. Turjan, A., Kienhuis, B., Deprettere, E.: An integer linear programming approach to classify the communication in process networks. In: Schepers, H. (ed.) SCOPES 2004. LNCS, vol. 3199, pp. 62–76. Springer, Heidelberg (2004). https://doi.org/10.1007/978-3-540-30113-4_6
13. Turjan, A., Kienhuis, B., Deprettere, E.F.: Translating affine nested-loop programs to process networks. In: Proceedings of the International Conference on Compilers, Architectures and Synthesis for Embedded Systems (CASES), pp. 220–229. ACM, New York (2004)
14. Verdoolaege, S., Nikolov, H., Stefanov, T.: PN: a tool for improved derivation of process networks. EURASIP J. Adv. Sig. Process. **2007**(1), 1–13 (2007)
15. van der Wolf, P., et al.: Design and programming of embedded multiprocessors: an interface-centric approach. In: Proceedings of the International Conference on Hardware-Software Codesign and System Synthesis (CODES+ISSS), pp. 206–217. ACM, New York (2004)

A Hardware-Accelerated Estimation-Based Power Profiling Unit - Enabling Early Power-Aware Embedded Software Design and On-Chip Power Management

Andreas Genser[1]([✉]), Christian Bachmann[1]([✉]), Christian Steger[1]([✉]), Reinhold Weiss[1]([✉]), and Josef Haid[2]([✉])

[1] Institute for Technical Informatics, Graz University of Technology, Inffeldgasse 16/I, 8010 Graz, Austria
{andreas.genser,christian.bachmann,steger,rweiss}@tugraz.at
[2] Infineon Technologies Austria AG, Design Center Graz, Graz, Austria
josef.haid@infineon.com
http://www.iti.tugraz.at, http://www.infineon.com

Abstract. The power consumption of battery powered and energy scavenging devices has become a major design metric for embedded systems. Increasingly complex software applications as well as rising demands in operating times, while having restricted power budgets are main drivers of power-aware system design as well as power management techniques. Within this work, a hardware-accelerated estimation-based power profiling unit delivering real-time power information has been developed. Power consumption feedback to the designer allows for real-time power analysis of embedded systems. Power saving potential as well as power-critical events can be identified in much less time compared to power simulations. Hence, the designer can take countermeasures already at early design stages, which enhances development efficiency and decreases time-to-market. Moreover, this work forms the basis for estimation-based on-chip power management by leveraging the power information for adoptions on system frequency and supply voltage in order to enhance the power efficiency of embedded systems. Power estimation accuracies achieved for a deep sub-micron smart-card controller are above 90% compared to gate-level simulations.

1 Introduction

Rising complexity of embedded software applications and the advance in processing power available in embedded systems require power analysis techniques to identify power saving potential. Furthermore, the system stability of energy scavenging devices (e.g., contact-less smart-cards) may suffer from power critical events, such as power peaks, hence their detection and prevention is of great importance in order to ensure reliable system operation.

© Springer-Verlag GmbH Germany, part of Springer Nature 2019
P. Stenström et al. (Eds.): Transactions on HiPEAC V, LNCS 11225, pp. 59–78, 2019.
https://doi.org/10.1007/978-3-662-58834-5_4

Among all abstraction layers the greatest power saving potential can be identified on the application layer [1]. To enable the design of power-efficient software applications, power consumption feedback to the software designer should be available already at early design stages. However, commercially available power estimation and analysis tools are often operating on low abstraction layers, which are usually not available to the software designer. Low-level power simulations lead to extensive run-times, which make power evaluations for complex designs unfeasible. Consequently, high abstraction level power information at early design stages is highly desirable from a software designer's point of view. Alongside the ability to identify power saving potential, it also offers the early detection of potential power bugs.

Functional hardware emulation by means of prototyping platforms, such as FPGA-boards, has become a widespread technique for functional verification. Power information, however, is still in many cases gathered by power simulators. In this work, which is part of the PowerHouse[1] project, we propose a hardware-accelerated estimation-based real-time power profiling approach to circumvent this limitation. A given design augmented with power estimation hardware allows for obtaining power alongside functional characteristics in real-time. Power saving potential or power peaks can hence be detected earlier in the design cycle, which normally is not feasible before the design is available in silicon and actual physical measurements can be carried out.

By coupling this approach with a software development environment, valuable power information can be transferred to the software designer. This concept is depicted in Fig. 1. The FPGA-platform collects functional verification and power characteristics information, which are transmitted to a host computer. These information can be evaluated and visualized in a software development environment.

The proposed hardware-accelerated estimation-based power profiling unit forms also the basis for estimation-based on-chip power management. By providing instantaneous power information, system frequency as well as supply voltage levels are adapted by the system autonomously to present power availability conditions. Particularly in the contact-less smart-card domain, power management techniques to smoothen the power profile can help to minimize power peaks and to prevent power bugs.

This paper is structured as follows. Section 2 provides information on previous work. Section 3 briefly shows our research contributions. In Sect. 4 the design of the real-time power profiling unit is discussed. Section 5 outlines a case-study applying the concepts developed in this work to a contact-less deep sub-micron smart-card controller, while Sect. 6 covers the concept of estimation-based power management on the basis of the proposed power profiling unit. Finally, conclusions drawn from the current work and future activities are summarized in Sect. 7.

---

[1] Project partners are Infineon Technologies Austria AG, Austria Card GmbH and TU Graz. The project is funded by the Austrian Federal Ministry for Transport, Innovation, and Technology under the FIT-IT contract FFG 815193.

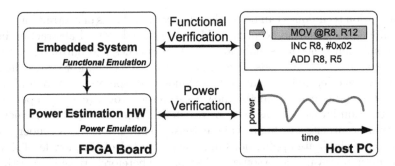

Fig. 1. Overview of the estimation-based power profiling approach for power-aware embedded software design comprising host computer interaction and visualization [2]

2 Related Work

Power profiling for embedded software can be categorized in (i) *measurement-based* and (ii) *estimation-based* methods.

Measurement-based methods are performed by taking actual physical measurements. This yields high accuracy compared to other approaches but requires additional measurement-equipment.

In contrast, power profiling by means of *estimation methods* is often based on power modeling. These techniques are usually less accurate but provide greater flexibility, since also power consumption for sub-modules of the system can be derived. In the following we compare ongoing research activities in the field of power profiling.

2.1 Measurement-Based Methods

In [3], PowerScope an energy profiling tool for mobile applications is introduced. The system's current consumption is automatically measured during run-time by a digital multimeter. Measurement data are collected for later analysis on a host computer.

An oscilloscope measurement-based profiling technique is proposed by Texas Instruments in [4]. The current drawn by a DSP system is profiled and results are visualized on a host computer in TI's software development environment.

2.2 Estimation-Based Methods

Power profiling by means of estimation techniques can be subdivided into (i) *simulation-based* and (ii) *hardware-accelerated* approaches.

Simulation-based power estimation executes programs on simulators to obtain circuit activity information. Power values are acquired based on these information. In hardware-accelerated power estimation approaches, power information is derived from power models, which are implemented in hardware.

Estimation techniques can be employed on various levels of abstraction resulting in different estimation accuracies. Moreover, the degree of abstraction influences simulation times for simulation-based approaches and hardware-effort for hardware-accelerated methods. Real-time power estimation, however, is limited to hardware-accelerated estimation techniques that operate on a high abstraction level. Commercially available power estimation tools (e.g. [5]) operate on low abstraction levels, such as gate- or register-transfer level (RTL). Achievable estimation accuracies are high, while extensive simulation times render power estimation of elaborate applications unfeasible. On top of this, low-level simulators are often not available to software designers. Therefore, attempts to estimate the system's power consumption on a higher level of abstraction are carried out.

A *simulation-based* approach employing power models for instruction-level power estimations is proposed by Tiwari et al. in [6]. It allows for power and energy consumption estimation for given applications. The underlying power model considers the power consumption during instruction execution (i.e., base costs) and power consumption during the transition between instructions (i.e., circuit state overhead costs). In [7], Sami et al. consider additional microarchitectural effects to enhance the accuracy of instruction-level power estimation based on a pipeline-aware power model for very long instruction word (VLIW) architectures. A co-simulation based power estimation technique is introduced by Lajolo et al. in [8]. This approach for system on chips (SoCs) works on multiple abstraction levels. In principle, power estimation is performed on system level, while for refinement purposes and accuracy enhancements various components are co-simulated on lower levels of abstraction. Countermeasures against high simulation times are caching, statistical sampling and macro-modeling. A simulation framework for system-level SoC power estimation is introduced by Lee et al. in [9]. This approach is based on power models developed for the processor, memories and custom IP blocks. Power values derived are provided cycle-accurately to the designer in a dedicated profile-viewer. Ahuja et al. leverage a probabilistic RTL power estimation approach on system-level. To the expense of an accuracy loss of 3–9% they achieve simulation speedups of up to 12× compared to ordinary RTL power estimations [10].

Hardware-accelerated power estimation techniques are performed by augmenting the given system with existing or dedicated power estimation hardware. A power characterization process performed beforehand determines power values, which are mapped towards corresponding power states. For example, hardware events (e.g. CPU idle/run states, memory read/write states, etc.) are representatives of such power states. Available power estimation hardware can be extended to power state counters for energy consumption accounting. In [11], Bellosa gathers information by means of hardware event counters to derive thread-specific energy information for operating systems. Joseph et al. obtain the power consumption of a system by exploiting existing hardware performance counters of a microcontroller [12]. Microprocessor performance counters are utilized for system-wide power estimations by Bircher et al. in [13]. A power macro-model based coprocessor approach for energy accounting is proposed in [14]. Energy events identified by energy sensors are tracked by a central controller. In general, the additional power estimation hardware requires extra chip area but yields also a speed-up compared to simulation-based approaches.

Power emulation represents a special case of hardware-accelerated power estimation. FPGA-boards can be used as a typical prototyping platform to emulate not only the functional system behavior but also its power consumption. A given system comprising power estimation hardware is mapped onto an FPGA-platform. Functional verification and power estimation can be performed in real-time even before the silicon implementation of the system is available.

Coburn et al. presented an overview of the power emulation principle in [15]. Run-time improvements by power estimation hardware-acceleration of about 10× to 500× over commercial power estimation tools are achieved. Strategies to minimize the hardware overhead introduced by power estimation hardware are proposed. In [16], this approach is extended to a hybrid power estimation methodology for complex SoCs. This framework combines simulation and emulation techniques, which significantly reduce power analysis times. In [17], the power consumption of processor cores is estimated employing power emulation to guide process migration between cores.

3 Contributions

Power profiling by means of physical measurements is typically very coarse-grained and limited to the entire chip due to chip integration and packaging. Moreover, the final chip is not available at early design stages.

Simulation-based power profiling techniques can be employed at the beginning of the design cycle, however they are rendered unfeasible for complex applications due to extensive simulation times. To encourage the software designer to consider power aspects at early design stages, we propose a hardware-accelerated estimation-based power profiling unit delivering power consumption information in real-time. Power information is delivered to the software designer before silicon is available by utilizing an FPGA prototyping platform comprising power estimation hardware (power emulation). Expensive redesigns caused by power bugs can be avoided, which helps to decrease time-to-market (see Fig. 2).

An automatic measure to increase system reliability is offered by on-chip power management based on our proposed hardware-accelerated estimation-based power profiling unit. The autonomous adoption of system frequency and supply voltage implies power profile smoothening that minimizes the harmfulness of power peaks. Thus, the proposed power profiling unit provides a promising approach for increasing system stability in power critical applications as well as for enhancing the system's power efficiency in general.

The main goals of this work can be defined as follows:

- Deliver power information to the designer at early design stages to allow for:
  - Power-efficient software application design
  - Power-critical event detection

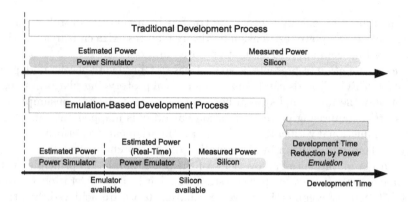

Fig. 2. Emulation-based vs. traditional power profiling approach [2]

– Enabling hardware-accelerated estimation-based on-chip power management for gaining power efficiency and to enhance the reliability of power critical embedded systems applications.

4 Design of a Hardware-Accelerated Estimation-Based Power Profiling Unit

Estimation-based power profiling methods derive power information by exploiting power models. The abstraction layer on which these models are set up determines model complexity and estimation accuracy. Low-level models established on transistor- or gate-level are complex and require extensive hardware resources. Hence, they are not suitable for hardware-accelerated estimation-based power profiling. In contrast, on a higher abstraction layer only main system components (e.g. CPU, memory, coprocessor, etc.) are taken into account. This leads to more compact models, hence real-time power profiling with moderate area increases is only feasible following this approach.

4.1 Power Model

Power models on a high level of abstraction are often based on linear regression methods. Details can be obtained in [18] and implementations are discussed in [6] and [19]. A linear regression model can be defined as

$$\hat{y} = \sum_{i=0}^{n-1} c_i x_i + \epsilon. \tag{1}$$

$\mathbf{x} = [x_1, x_2, \ldots x_{n-1}]$ gives the vector of model parameters. x_i represent system states, such as CPU modes (e.g., idle, run) or memory accesses (e.g., read, write). The vector of model coefficients can be written as $\mathbf{c} = [c_1, c_2, \ldots c_{n-1}]^T$.

Each model coefficient c_i contains power information and has to be determined during a power model characterization process. The linear combination of model parameters $\mathbf{x}$ and model coefficients $\mathbf{c}$ forms the power estimate $\hat{y}$. The deviation between the real power value y and its estimate $\hat{y}$ is stated by ϵ (i.e., the estimation error).

4.2 Power Characterization Process

Typically a linear regression model can be designed in three major steps.

(i) *Selection of model parameters.* The choice of model parameters directly influences the model's accuracy and is therefore of great importance. In addition, the cross-correlation between model parameters reflects the amount of redundancy in the model. This metric helps to keep a model as small as possible and thus compact in terms of hardware resources.

(ii) *Selection of the training-set.* The training-set is based on m power measurements for a number of m vectors $\mathbf{x^i}$, each of which containing n model parameters

$$\mathbf{x^i} = [x_0^i, x_1^i, \ldots x_{n-1}^i] \text{ for } 0 \leq i \leq m - 1. \tag{2}$$

Vectors $\mathbf{x^i}$ can be combined to the matrix

$$\mathbf{X} = [\mathbf{x^0}, \mathbf{x^1}, \ldots \mathbf{x^{m-1}}]^\mathbf{T}. \tag{3}$$

Power values y acquired by low abstraction level power simulations (e.g., gate-level simulations) or physical measurements for corresponding vectors $\mathbf{x^i}$ can be expressed as

$$\mathbf{y} = [y_0, y_1, \ldots y_{m-1}]^T. \tag{4}$$

Finally, $\mathbf{X}$ and $\mathbf{y}$ define the training-set given as the tuple $\mathbf{T}$ in (5).

$$\mathbf{T} = (\mathbf{y}, \mathbf{X}) \tag{5}$$

The linear regression model given in (1) can also be written in matrix-form, which is depicted in (6).
$$\mathbf{y} = \mathbf{Xc} \tag{6}$$

Vectors $\mathbf{x^i}$ in $\mathbf{X}$ are derived from test applications (micro-benchmarks) on a given embedded system and corresponding power values $\mathbf{y}$ are determined by gate-level simulations or physical power measurements.

(iii) *Least squares fit method.* The number of elements in the training-set $\mathbf{T}$ is usually much higher than the number of model parameters $\mathbf{c}$. This implies that the number of rows in $\mathbf{y}$ and the number of columns in $\mathbf{X}$ is higher than actually required to solve the linear system of equations in (6). Hence, the system is overdetermined and no exact solution exists. To overcome this issue model parameters are determined, while minimizing the square error by using the least squares fit method.

The impact of different power model setup strategies on the estimation accuracy has been explored in our previous work [20]. Starting from (i) a *manual model*, i.e., model parameters are selected manually, accuracy enhancements could be achieved by performing (ii) a *naive brute force* method that carries out linear regression with the entire large set of model parameters of the system; (iii) an *intra-signal correlation* method that removes signals stuck at a logical level or that do not show any switching activity; and (iv) a *power-signal activity filter* that computes the cross-correlation between model parameters and the transient power profile. By means of these methods, the average estimation error could be reduced from 11.78% for the *manual model* to 4.71% for a model built upon the combination of *intra-signal correlation* and the *power-signal activity filter*.

4.3   Power Estimation Architecture

The power estimation (PE) architecture that integrates the power model in hardware is illustrated in Fig. 3.

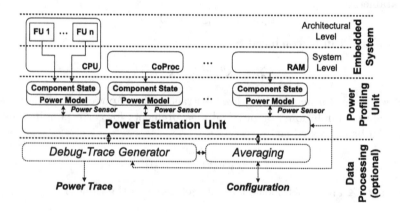

Fig. 3. Power estimation architecture, obtained and adopted from [2]

Power sensors are employed to track state information of system modules. For accuracy purposes also lower abstraction layer information can be considered (e.g., state information of functional units of the CPU). State-dependant power information are stored in a software-configurable table that is integrated in the power sensors. These state information are mapped towards power values using a table-lookup approach. Figure 4 depicts the principle structure of a power sensor module.

Each of a number of k power sensors covers l system states and contributes to the entire power model as expressed in (7). The PE-architecture delivers power information each cycle, hence time-dependency t is introduced in the following equations to account for power values estimated at different points in time.

$$y_{j,i}(t) = c_i\, x_i(t) \text{ for } 0 \leq i \leq l-1 \ \wedge \ 0 \leq j \leq k-1 \qquad (7)$$

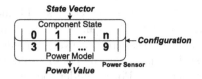

Fig. 4. Power sensor [2]

16-bit registers are provided to configure the power sensors with the power coefficients information obtained from **c**. It is worth noting that this power table can also be reconfigured during program run-time. This enables the masking of system modules, allowing the tracking of the power consumption of single sub-modules.

The power estimation unit accumulates 16-bit power sensor outputs according to (8). This constitutes an instantaneous, cycle-accurate up to 32-bit wide power estimate $y(t)$ for the overall system. The entirety of power sensors comprising the power estimation unit represent the power model established in hardware (see equality in (1) and (8)).

$$y(t) = \sum_{j=0}^{k-1}\sum_{i=0}^{l-1} y_{j,i}(t) = \sum_{i=0}^{n-1} c_i\, x_i(t) \tag{8}$$

Further post-processing is applied by the averaging module, which allows for smoothing and de-noising of a sequence of power values. This is enabled by a configurable moving average filter as shown in (9). Filtering properties can be changed by adjusting N.

$$y_{avg} = \frac{1}{N} \sum_{j=0}^{N-1} y(t-j) \tag{9}$$

Finally, the debug-trace generator module assembles trace messages out of the power information that are transferred to a host computer for evaluation purposes and further processing. Note that the averaging and the debug-trace generator module are optional. They are only required for the power-aware embedded software design approach and can be omitted for on-chip power management.

4.4   Design Flow

Figure 5 outlines the design flow of the estimation-based real-time power profiling approach. A synthesizeable RTL-model of the target system forms the basis for the characterization process. After synthesis gate-level simulations based on micro-benchmarks are performed and activity information as well as power profiles are acquired based on value change dump (VCD) files. These information is fed to a power modeling process, deriving power model coefficients.

The target system's and the PE-architecture's RTL-models are merged for the generation of a single netlist. This can either be a netlist for an FPGA-platform to allow for estimation-based power-aware embedded software design or a netlist for chip synthesis incorporating the power profiling unit for estimation-based on-chip power management. Power model coefficients determined beforehand are used to configure the power sensors for tailoring the PE-architecture to the given target system.

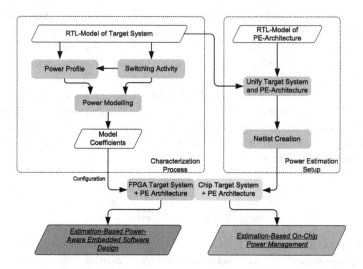

Fig. 5. Design flow allowing for two possible applications: (i) estimation-based real-time power profiling for enabling power-aware embedded software design, (ii) estimation-based on-chip power management

4.5   System Set-Up

Power model coefficients obtained during the characterization process deliver configuration data for the power sensors. Listing 1.1 illustrates how to configure power sensors to tailor them to the power consumption of system modules. 16-bit registers are provided for this purpose.

```
// start of program

//configuration of power sensor1
PWRSEN0_STATE0 = 0x005A;   //CPU run mode
PWRSEN0_STATE1 = 0x0011;   //CPU halt mode
PWRSEN0_STATE2 = 0x0013;   //CPU sleep mode

//configuration of power sensor2
PWRSEN1_STATE0 = 0x0013;   //memory read
```

```
PWRSEN1_STATE1 = 0x001A;    //memory write
...

activate_power_estimation ();

start_main_program ();
```

Listing 1.1. Power estimation set-up, power sensor configuration

A variable number of system states for a variable number of system modules can be configured with power coefficients. Finally, power profiling is activated before normal application execution starts. The run-time overhead introduced due to power sensor configuration is negligible compared to the number of cycles executed by a typical application. A debug-trace message containing power information is automatically generated and transferred to the host computer for power information evaluation and profile visualization without the interaction of the software designer.

If power analysis of sub-modules of the system is desired, the power sensor attached to the module of interest is configured as illustrated in Listing 1.1. The configuration of the remaining modules is skipped, so they do not contribute to the overall power consumption.

For on-chip power management, the abovementioned power sensor configuration process is done in hardware by hardwiring power consumption information held by the power sensors.

5 Case Study: Profiling of Power-Critical Smart-Card Applications

Smart-card applications have been penetrating manifold market segments in the last years. Access control, electronic passport or payment are only a few out of many existing applications. Smart-cards can be categorized in (i) *contact-based* and (ii) *contact-less* derivatives. Contact-based smart-cards are powered if inserted into a reader device, while contact-less systems consume power via an RF-field generated by the reader device. Therefore, contact-less devices are subjected to stringent power limitations.

Figure 6 illustrates the coupling of the reader device with the contact-less smart-card by a magnetic field H. A certain amount of power is transferred from the reader device to the smart-card at a time. The transferable power is limited, hence exceeding a maximum power limit due to power-peaks causes supply voltage drops that in turn can affect system stability if the supply voltage falls below a certain voltage limit $V_{DD_{critical}}$. This case-study demonstrates the capability of our estimation-based power profiling approach to support the software designer early in the development process to avoid such worst-case scenarios.

5.1 Smart-Card Architecture Overview

Figure 7 depicts a typical contact-less smart-card system. It is based on a 16-bit pipelined cache architecture comprising a memory encryption/decryption

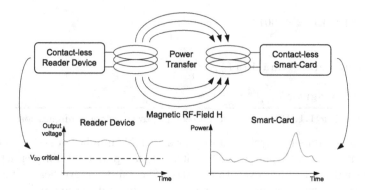

Fig. 6. Power supply of a contact-less smart card by a magnetic field generated by a reader device

(MED) unit and volatile and non-volatile memories. Cryptographic coprocessors are included for Advanced Encryption Standard (AES), Data Encryption Standard (DES) and RSA algorithm acceleration. Moreover peripherals, such as timers or a random number generator (RNG) are provided. For communication purposes a number of interfaces (i.e., UART, I2C, contact-less interface) exist. System modules are powered by an externally generated RF-field. Energy is collected by an antenna system and power supply conditioning and stabilization by means of an analog front-end are carried out.

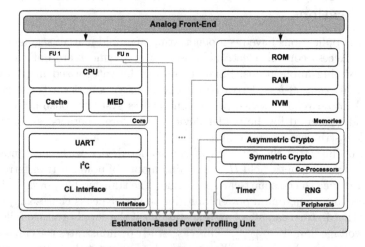

Fig. 7. Block diagram of a typical contact-less smart-card system incorporating the estimation-based power profiling unit

System modules that are major contributors to the overall power consumption are identified during a power characterization process. Moreover, available operating modes of each system module influencing the amount of power consumed are considered during this characterization process. A number of micro-benchmarks in order to test many of these operating modes were applied. Based on the result of the characterization process, power model coefficients were obtained to configure the power sensors as shown in Listing 1.1. Table 1 summarizes system modules and corresponding operating modes considered for the power model.

Table 1. Operating modes of typical smart-card components considered in the power model

Unit	Mode(s)
CPU	run, halt
MED	encryption, decryption
Cache	read, write (hit, miss)
Memories	read, write
UART	read, write
Peripherals	on, off
Coproc.	encryption: AES128/192/256, (Single-, Double-, Triple-) DES
Coproc.	decryption: AES128/192/256 (Single-, Double-, Triple-) DES

5.2 Payment Application Profile Analysis

A typical application for smart-cards incorporating a symmetric cryptographic coprocessor is payment. Payment applications usually contain authentication procedures requiring cryptographic operations. Figure 8 illustrates a power-relevant section of a typical power profile of a future payment application obtained with our estimation-based power profiling approach. The figure shows two distinct power peaks. The first one marks the power consumption of AES encryption computations, while the second peak results from AES decryption computations.

We assume that the maximum available power provided by the RF-field is 0.9 as shown in Fig. 8 (note that power values are normalized for confidentiality reasons). Hence, the payment application execution would fail due to power peaks caused by coprocessor operation.

If not obvious to the designer at this step, the source of the power peaks can be identified by decomposing the smart-card system into sub-modules. Power profiles for sub-modules are acquired by reconfiguring the power sensors. Figure 9 depicts power profile results for the smart-card's CPU, cache (both incorporated in the core) and the coprocessors decomposed for sub-module power profile analysis. As a reference also the accumulated power profile that indicates the overall power consumption is shown.

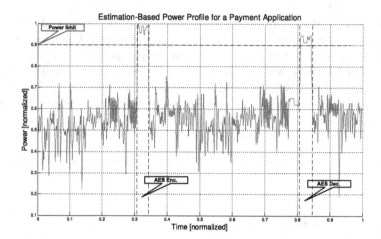

Fig. 8. Power-relevant section of a payment application power profile obtained by estimation-based power profiling (power exceeds affordable level)

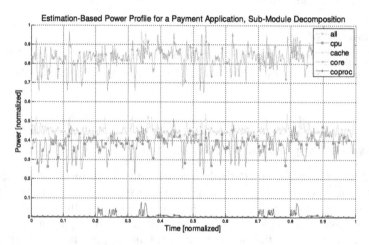

Fig. 9. Payment application power profile decomposed for sub-module power analysis

Major contributors to the overall power consumption for the given example are obviously CPU, cache and the coprocessor, when active. Peripherals, communication interfaces and also memories are inactive during the considered time frame of the payment application and therefore do not add to the system's power consumption. It can be clearly observed that the coprocessor's power consumption causes the overall power profile to exceed the absolute maximum power of 0.9.

Various countermeasures could be taken to circumvent this issue. The AES algorithm could be implemented in software to avoid using coprocessor acceleration. An alternative is also to reduce the system's clock frequency. Figure 10 shows the power profile when scaling down the system frequency from 33 MHz to

28 MHz. Power peaks are scaled down below 0.9, hence frequency scaling resolves the power peak issue. Both remedies come at the cost of reducing the payment application's performance, but they ensure reliable operation.

The system's power consumption can also be reduced by exploiting CPU low-power features during the critical peak phase. During coprocessor activity the CPU as a main power consumer is shut down and reactivated after the coprocessor has finished execution. Power peaks can be avoided by applying this counter-measure without degrading the system's performance. Figure 11 illustrates the effect of the CPU low-power implementation.

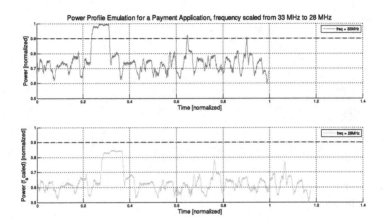

Fig. 10. Payment application power profile obtained by estimation-based power profiling (stable system operation due to frequency-scaling)

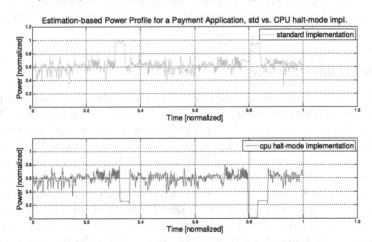

Fig. 11. Payment application power profile obtained by estimation-based power profiling (stable system operation due to CPU low-power features exploitation)

5.3 Accuracy of Estimation-Based Power Profiling

Figure 12 shows power profiles of the payment application. A comparison between the estimation-based power profiling result and gate-level power simulation profiles obtained with *Magma Blastfusion 5.2.2* [21] is given.

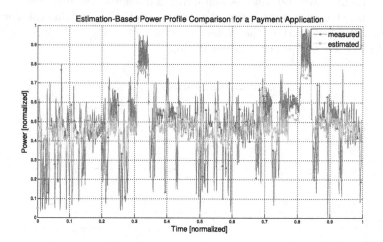

Fig. 12. Power profile comparison, gate-level power simulation profile vs. estimation-based power profile

Accuracy considerations for other executed test applications are summarized in Table 2. The relative power error on average and the corresponding variance are given. For all tested applications relative average power errors are less than 10%.

5.4 Performance Evaluation

One of the major advantages of the hardware-accelerated estimation-based power profiling approach is the capability to acquire power profiles in real-time. Power estimation takes no longer than application execution on the target-system. Hence, the power profile is available immediately after execution. Table 3 shows execution times of power profile simulations on a gate-level basis using *Magma Blastfusion* compared to our estimation-based approach. Simulation times are depicted compared to hardware-accelerated power estimation run-times. Power estimation of the payment application takes 136 μs, whereas the power simulation is about 17 h. Hence, our approach shows that extensively high simulation times can be reduced enormously by means of the hardware-accelerated estimation-based power profiling unit.

It is obvious that power simulation of complex applications is rendered unfeasible due to far too extensive simulation times. Therefore, power saving potential or power peaks leading to system failure cannot be detected at an early design

Table 2. Power estimation accuracy comparison for a number of executed micro-benchmarks

Algorithm	Duration (μs)	# Cycles	Error (%)			
			Power			Energy
			Avg.	σ^2		
ALU	69.5	2293	4.9	0.9		3.1
Cache	120.5	3978	2.2	2		0.5
Dhrystone	126.5	4176	3.9	2.7		1.4
Memory	52.1	1722	−6.1	1.3		−7.8
Payment (Coproc., CPU halt)	136	4510	5.7	3.8		1.6
Payment (Coproc., CPU run)	146.6	4837	2.2	2.9		−0.5
DES (Coproc., CPU halt)	87.8	2899	5.3	4		1.8
DES (Coproc., CPU run)	93.1	3072	4.5	3.9		1.1

Table 3. Performance comparison of power profiling, simulation vs. hardware-accelerated estimation-based approach

Algorithm	# Cycles	Duration	
		Simulation (h)[a]	Estimation-based (μs)
ALU	2293	4.1	69.5
Cache	3978	14.9	120.5
Dhrystone	4176	18.6	126.5
Memory	1722	5.9	52.1
Payment (Coproc., CPU halt)	4510	17.8	136
Payment (Coproc., CPU run)	4837	23.8	146.6
DES (Coproc., CPU halt)	2899	9.5	87.8
DES (Coproc., CPU run)	3072	10.2	93.1

[a]Simulation has been performed on a state of the art server system. The sampling rate at which power simulations have been performed is 33 MHz, which is the clock frequency of the smart-card system.

stage. By means of the hardware-accelerated estimation-based power profiling approach, power estimates are available immediately and already when working with FPGA prototyping platforms. Countermeasures to circumvent power peaks can be taken before the device is available in silicon and physical measurements can be performed.

5.5   Resource Allocation

The smart-card system incorporating the PE-architecture has been synthesized on an *Altera Stratix II FPGA* [22]. For power estimation purposes additional

1.5% of hardware is added to the overall system for a power model consisting of 40 model parameters. In Table 4, the resource allocation of different units of the PE-architecture is shown. The largest portion of resources is occupied by the system bus interface together with the power tables load mechanism as well as by the power sensors and the power estimation unit. For a more complex power model, power sensor and power estimation resources are expected to grow linearly with the number of model parameters.

Table 4. Composition of the amount of combinational and register resources allocated by the PE-architecture on an *Altera Stratix II FPGA*

	Combinational logic (%)	Registers (%)
Bus IF, load mechanism[a]	32.6	7.2
Pwr. sensors, PE unit	58.1	78.5
Averaging	5.4	10.7
Debug-Trace gen.	3.9	3.6

[a]The PE-architecture is interfaced to the system bus allowing for memory-mapped power sensor configuration via register accesses

6   Concept for Estimation-Based On-Chip Power Management

Power management has emerged as an effective technique to gain power and energy efficiency in embedded systems. The system is dynamically reconfigured during run-time to provide the requested system performance under the consideration of given power constraints. System reconfiguration can either be accomplished by switching off unused system components or by dynamic voltage and frequency scaling (DVFS). In the latter case, system adoption is carried out by dynamically changing system frequency and supply voltage levels.

The concept of estimation-based power management is illustrated in Fig. 13 by means of a smart-card use-case. The hardware-accelerated estimation-based power profiling unit is integrated on-chip together with the smart-card system. Power consumption information is provided cycle-accurately and in real-time to a power manager that autonomously adopts system frequency and supply voltage in order to smoothen the power profile. Alongside making a system more power-efficient, we assume that DVFS power management can be an effective measure for energy scavenging devices to make them more robust against power peaks.

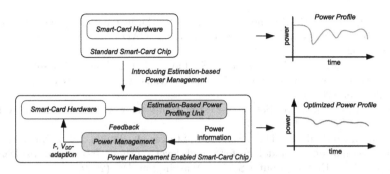

Fig. 13. Power management principle based on the hardware-accelerated estimation-based power profiling unit

7   Conclusions and Future Work

Extensive run-times of power simulators render power analysis of increasingly complex embedded systems unfeasible. The hardware-accelerated estimation-based power profiling approach proposed in this work, delivers power information to the software designer in real-time. Moreover, by employing FPGA prototyping platforms, these power information is available already at early design stages. The proposed power profiling unit has proven to be an effective option to estimate the system's power consumption and to deliver power information with accuracies of above 90% on average. This paves the way for power-efficient embedded software design and the capability to cope with and to avoid power critical events during the design phase more efficiently.

In our future work, we will focus on power management by leveraging power consumption information of our developed power profiling unit. Power management policies enhancing the system's power efficiency as well as reducing the risk of malfunctions due to power peaks is going to be the focus of our prospective research.

References

1. Macii, E., Poncino, M.: Power macro-models for high-level power estimation. In: Piguet, C. (ed.) Low-Power Electronics Design, pp. 39-1–39-18. CRC Press, Boca Raton (2005). Chap. 39
2. Genser, A., Bachmann, C., Haid, J., Steger, C., Weiss, R.: An emulation-based real-time power profiling unit for embedded software. In: SAMOS, pp. 67–73 (2009)
3. Flinn, J., Satyanarayanan, M.: PowerScope: a tool for profiling the energy usage of mobile applications. In: WMCSA, pp. 2–10 (1999)
4. Texas Instruments: Analyzing Target System Energy Consumption in Code Composer Studio[TM] IDE (2002)
5. Flynn, J., Waldo, B.: Power management in complex SoC design. Technical report, Synopsys Inc. White Paper (2005)
6. Tiwari, V., Malik, S., Wolfe, A.: Power analysis of embedded software: a first step towards software power minimization. In: ICCAD, pp. 384–390 (1994)

7. Sami, M., Sciuto, D., Silvano, C., Zaccaria, V.: An instruction-level energy model for embedded VLIW architectures. IEEE Trans. CAD Integr. Circ. Syst. **21**, 998–1010 (2002)
8. Lajolo, M., Raghunathan, A., Dey, S., Lavagno, L.: Cosimulation-based power estimation for system-on-chip design. IEEE Trans. Very Large Scale Integr. Syst. **10**, 253–266 (2002)
9. Lee, I., et al.: PowerViP: SoC power estimation framework at transaction level. In: ASP-DAC, pp. 551–558 (2006)
10. Ahuja, S., Mathaikutty, D.A., Singh, G., Stetzer, J., Shukla, S.K., Dingankar, A.: Power estimation methodology for a high-level synthesis framework. In: ISQED, pp. 541–546. IEEE Computer Society, Washington, DC (2009)
11. Bellosa, F.: The benefits of event: driven energy accounting in power-sensitive systems. In: SIGOPS European Workshop, pp. 37–42 (2000)
12. Joseph, R., Martonosi, M.: Run-time power estimation in high performance microprocessors. In: ISLPED, pp. 135–140 (2001)
13. Bircher, W.L., John, L.K.: Complete system power estimation: a trickle-down approach based on performance events. In: ISPASS, pp. 158–168, April 2007
14. Haid, J., Kaefer, G., Steger, Ch., Weiss, R.: Run-time energy estimation in system-on-a-chip designs. In: ASP-DAC, pp. 595–599 (2003)
15. Coburn, J., Ravi, S., Raghunathan, A.: Power emulation: a new paradigm for power estimation. In: DAC, pp. 700–705 (2005)
16. Ghodrat, M.A., Lahiri, K., Raghunathan, A.: Accelerating system-on-chip power analysis using hybrid power estimation. In: DAC, pp. 883–886 (2007)
17. Bhattacharjee, A., Contreras, G., Martonosi, M.: Full-system chip multiprocessor power evaluations using FPGA-based emulation. In: ISLPED, pp. 335–340 (2008)
18. Bogliolo, A., Benini, L., De Micheli, G.: Regression-based RTL power modeling. ACM Trans. Des. Autom. Electron. Syst. **5**, 337–372 (2000)
19. Krintz, C., Gurun, S.: A run-time, feedback-based energy estimation model for embedded devices. In: CODES+ISSS, pp. 28–33 (2006)
20. Bachmann, C., Genser, A., Steger, C., Weiss, R., Haid, J.: Automated power characterization for run-time power emulation of SoC designs. In: DSD (2010, in press)
21. Magma Design Automation Inc.: Blastfusion, July 2010. http://www.magma-da.com/
22. Altera Coroporation: Stratix II, July 2010. http://www.altera.com/

The Abstract Streaming Machine: Compile-Time Performance Modelling of Stream Programs on Heterogeneous Multiprocessors

Paul M. Carpenter$^{(\boxtimes)}$ (iD), Alex Ramirez, and Eduard Ayguade

Barcelona Supercomputing Center, C/Jordi Girona, 31, 08034 Barcelona, Spain
{paul.carpenter,alex.ramirez,eduard.ayguade}@bsc.es

Abstract. Stream programming is a promising step towards portable, efficient, correct use of parallelism. A stream program is built from kernels that communicate only through point-to-point streams. The stream compiler maps a portable stream program onto the target, automatically sizing communications buffers and applying optimizing transformations such as blocking, task fission and task fusion.

This paper presents the Abstract Streaming Machine (ASM), the machine description and performance model used by the ACOTES stream compiler. We explain how the parameters of the ASM and the ASM coarse-grain simulator are used by the partitioning and queue length assignment phases of the ACOTES compiler. Our experiments on the Cell Broadband Engine show that the predictions from the ASM have a maximum relative error of 15% across our benchmarks.

1 Introduction

As the industry moves towards multiprocessors, there is a growing need for software that exploits concurrency [2]. Many embedded systems provide multiple processors, often with multiple ISAs or microarchitectures to optimize for diverse applications and mitigate Amdahl's law [3,4]; e.g. TI OMAP [5], ARM MPCore [6], Intel IXP2850 [7], Nexperia Home Platform [8], and ST Nomadik [9]. Many embedded systems [5,10] and the Cell Broadband Engine (CBE) [11] provide distributed memory, which has lower power consumption and higher storage density than shared memory, but it is harder to program. Different types of applications contain different kinds of parallelism, which may need to be expressed in different ways [12].

One important class of applications comprises multimedia, graphics and signal processing. These applications can be represented as *stream programs*, in which independent blocks communicate and synchronize only via regular streams of data. Such a representation exposes task and data parallelism that would be

---

This article is an extended version of a paper presented at SAMOS 2009 [1].

© Springer-Verlag GmbH Germany, part of Springer Nature 2019
P. Stenström et al. (Eds.): Transactions on HiPEAC V, LNCS 11225, pp. 79–99, 2019.
https://doi.org/10.1007/978-3-662-58834-5_5

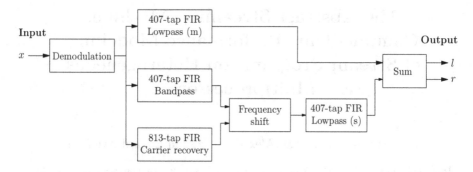

Fig. 1. Block diagram of an example stream program: GNU radio FM demodulation, showing seven kernels, connected by point-to-point streams

hidden if the program were written in C or a similar sequential programming language. Figure 1 is a graphical representation of our GNU radio FM demodulation program.

The key benefit of stream programming is that the stream compiler can perform high level transformations such as task fusion, fission and blocking. These transformations are necessary for good performance, and the right choice of transformations depends on the number and type of processors, the interconnect, and target topology.

The main contributions of this paper are:

- A novel simulation methodology for streaming applications,
- a flexible hardware description model,
- a flexible streaming application description model,
- and an explanation of how the ASM is used by two specific compiler optimizations in the ACOTES compiler.

2   The ACOTES Stream Compiler

This work is part of the ACOTES project[1] [13,14], which has been developing a complete open-source stream compiler for embedded systems. The ACOTES compiler partitions a stream program to use task-level parallelism, aggregates communications through blocking, and statically allocates communications buffers. The stream program is written using the Stream Programming Model (SPM) [15,16], an extension of C that uses pragma annotations to identify streaming tasks. If these pragmas are ignored, the result is a valid sequential program.

Figure 2 shows an example program using the SPM. The streaming part of a program is known as a *taskgroup*, and it comprises the loop following the acotes taskgroup pragma. This taskgroup has two *subtasks*, each of which contains

---

[1] Advanced Compiler Technologies for Embedded Streaming.

```
 1  int  main ()
 2  {
 3      char  c;
 4  #pragma acotes taskgroup
 5      while (fread(&c, sizeof(c), 1, stdin))
 6      {
 7  #pragma acotes task input(c) output(c)
 8          if ('A' <= c && c <= 'Z')
 9              c = c - 'A' + 'a';
10
11  #pragma acotes task input(c)
12          fwrite(&c, sizeof(c), 1, stdout);
13      }
14      return 0;
15  }
```

(a) SPM source code for tolower

(b) Streaming graph (flattened)

Fig. 2. Example SPM program from [14]

the statement or block following an **acotes task** pragma. The task's inputs and outputs are identified using the input and output clauses.

The SPM program begins running in a single thread. When execution reaches the taskgroup, the subtasks are created, and the program starts processing data in streams, passing inputs and outputs through the streams. More information can be found in the ACOTES documentation [15]. From the point of view of the mapping and queue sizing algorithms, the taskgroup and its subtasks have equal status, and are all known as *kernels*. This paper shows *flattened* stream graphs like Fig. 2(b), meaning that the hierarchical relationship between the taskgroup and its subtasks is ignored.

This paper describes the Abstract Streaming Machine (ASM), which represents the target system to the compiler. The ASM defines the target via coarse-grain simulation, since a closed-form analytical model is unlikely to capture the real behaviour of the program. This is because kernels can have variable execution times, and their relative firing rates can vary during the execution of the program—if they are inside conditional statements or loops.

Figure 3 shows the compilation flow. The source program is converted from SPM to C, using the Mercurium [17] source-to-source converter. This step translates pragma annotations into calls to the *acolib* run-time system, and inserts calls to the trace collection functions. It fuses kernels that are mapped to the same processor and inserts statically sized communication buffers, as required, between kernels on different processors. The mapping is determined by the search algorithm [18,19] (see Sect. 8). The resulting multi-threaded program is compiled using GCC, which has been extended within the ACOTES project to perform blocking, polyhedral transformations, and vectorization. Additional mapping information is provided to GCC using the Iterative Compilation Interface (ICI) [20]. The ACOTES compiler is iterative, meaning that the program may be compiled several times, as the search algorithm adjusts the mapping.

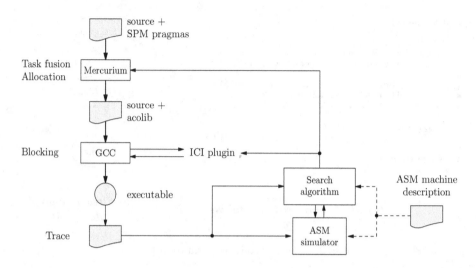

Fig. 3. The ACOTES iterative stream compiler

The *ASM simulator* executes a mapped stream program at a coarse granularity, and generates statistics which are used to improve the mapping. The inputs to the simulator are the *ASM machine description*, which describes the target, and the *ASM program model*, which describes the program. The ASM simulator is driven by a trace, which allows it to follow conditions and model varying computation times.

The ASM simulator is used inside the small feedback loop in the bottom right of Fig. 3; for example in determining the size of the stream buffers [18]. The trace format has been designed to allow a single trace to be reused for several different mappings. In Sect. 8 we describe in more detail the search algorithm and its interaction with the ASM.

3   Stream Programming and *acolib*

There are several definitions of stream programming, going back to the 1960s, differing mostly in the handling of control flow and restrictions on the program graph topology [21]. All stream programming models, however, represent the program as a set of *kernels*, communicating only via unidirectional *streams*. The producer on a stream has a blocking *push* primitive, which pushes an element on the stream, and the consumer has a blocking *pop* primitive. In the SPM, push and pop primitives are inserted at the boundaries between kernels, as indicated by the pragmas. This programming model is deterministic provided that the kernels themselves are deterministic, there is no other means of communication between kernels, each stream has one producer and one consumer, and the kernels cannot check whether a push or pop would block at a given time [22].

When the stream program is compiled, one or more kernels are mapped to each *task*, which is executed in its own thread. Tasks are managed by the

ACOTES run-time system, *acolib*, which uses POSIX pthreads or some other threading library. It creates and initializes tasks, manages communication, and waits for their completion.

Tasks communicate using four *acolib* communications primitives, which use a push model similar to the DBI (Direct Blocking In-order) variant of TTL [23]. These primitives push or pop *buffers*, which contain a fixed number of elements chosen by the compiler. The buffer sizes can be different at the producer and consumer ends, but the following description assumes they are the same, to avoid extraneous detail. A *block* is the contents of one buffer, and i and j count blocks, starting at zero. The first argument, s, is the stream. Each end of the stream has a fixed number of buffers, chosen by the compiler, and denoted $n_p(s)$ and $n_c(s)$.

ProducerAcquire(s, k). Wait for the producer buffer for block $i + k$ to be available, meaning that the DMA transfer of block $i + k - n_p(s)$ has completed

ProducerSend(s). Wait for the consumer buffer for block i to be available, meaning that the producer has received acknowledgement that block $i - n_c(s)$ has been discarded. Then send the block and increment i

ConsumerAcquire(s, k). Wait for block $j + k$ to arrive in the consumer buffer

ConsumerDiscard(s). Discard block j, send acknowledgement, and increment j.

4 ASM Machine Description

The target is represented as a undirected bipartite graph $H = (V, E)$ with *processors* and *memories* in one partition, and *interconnects* in the other. Figure 4 shows the topology of three example targets. The machine description defines the machine visible to software, provided by the OS and *acolib*, which may be different from the physical hardware. For example, the OS in a Playstation 3 makes six of the eight SPEs available to software, and does not make available the mapping from virtual to physical processor. We assume that the processors used by the stream program are not time-shared with other applications while the program is running.

Figure 5 shows the parameters used to characterize each resource in the system, together with their values for the Cell B.E. with the current *acolib*, and estimated values for an SMP. Each core has a separate definition, allowing the ASM to support both heterogeneous and homogeneous systems.

Each processor is defined using the parameters in Fig. 5(a). The details of the processor's ISA and micro-architecture are already described in the compiler's back-end, so are not duplicated in the ASM. The ASM processor description lists the costs of the *acolib* calls. The costs of ProducerSend and ConsumerAcquire are given by a staircase function; i.e. a fixed cost, a block size, and an incremental cost for each complete or partial block after the first. This variable cost is necessary both for FIFOs and for distributed memory with DMA. For distributed memory, the size of a single DMA transfer is often limited by hardware, so that larger transfers require additional processor time in ProducerSend to program multiple DMA transfers. The discontinuity at 16K in Fig. 11 is due to this effect.

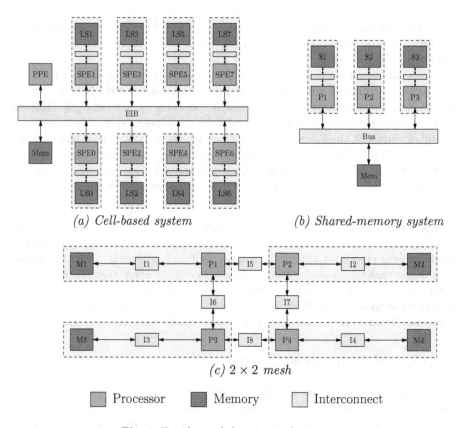

(a) Cell-based system   (b) Shared-memory system

(c) 2×2 mesh

▦ Processor   ▦ Memory   ▢ Interconnect

Fig. 4. Topology of three example targets

The addressSpace and hasIO parameters provide constraints on the compiler mapping, but are not required to evaluate the performance of a valid mapping. The former defines the local address space of the processor; i.e. which memories are directly accessible and where they appear in local virtual memory, and is used to place stream buffers. The model assumes that the dominant bus traffic is communication via streams, so either the listed memories are private local stores, or they are shared memories accessed via a private L1 cache. In the latter case, the cache should be sufficiently effective that the cache miss traffic on the interconnect is insignificant. The hasIO parameter defines which processors can perform system IO, and is a simple way to ensure that tasks that need system IO are mapped to a capable processor.

Each interconnect is defined using the parameters shown in Fig. 5(b). The system topology is given by the elements parameter, which for a given interconnect lists the adjacent processors and memories. Each interconnect is modelled as a bus with multiple channels, which has been shown to be a good approximation to the performance observed in practice when all processors and memories on a single link are equidistant [24]. If there are more messages than channels,

Parameter	Description	Cell	SMP
name	Unique name in platform namespace	'SPEn'	'CPUn'
clockRate	Clock rate, in GHz	3.2	2.4
hasIO	True if the processor can perform IO	False	True
addressSpace	List of the physical memories addressable by this processor and their virtual address	[(LSn,0)]	[('Mem',0)]
pushAcqCost	Cost, in cycles, to acquire a producer buffer (before waiting)	448	20
pushSendFixedCost	Fixed cost, in cycles, to push a block (before waiting)	1104	50
pushSendUnit	Number of bytes per push transfer unit	16384	0
pushSendUnitCost	Incremental cost, in cycles, to push pushUnit bytes	352	0
popAcqFixedCost	Fixed cost, in cycles, to pop a block (before waiting)	317	50
popAcqUnit	Number of bytes per pop transfer unit	16384	0
popAcqUnitCost	Incremental cost, in cycles, to pop popUnit bytes	0	0
popDiscCost	Cost, in cycles, to discard a consumer buffer (before waiting)	189	20

(a) *Definition of a processor*

Parameter	Description	Cell	SMP
name	Unique name in platform namespace	'EIB'	'FSB'
clockRate	Clock rate, in GHz	1.6	0.4
elements	List of the names of the elements (processors and memories) on the bus	['PPE', 'SPE0',···, 'SPE7']	['CPU0', ···, 'CPU3']
interfaceDuplex	If the bus has more than one channel, then define for each processor whether it can transmit and receive simultaneously on different channels	[True, ···, True]	[False, ···, False]
interfaceRouting	Define for each processor the type of routing from this bus: storeAndForward, cutThrough, or None	[None,···, None]	[None,···, None]
startLatency	Start latency, L, in cycles	80	0
startCost	Start cost on the channel, S, in cycles	0	0
bandwidthPerCh	Bandwidth per channel, B in bytes per cycle	16	16
finishCost	Finish cost, F, in cycles	0	0
numChannels	Number of channels on the bus	3	1
multiplexable	False for a hardware FIFO that can only support one stream	True	True

(b) *Definition of an interconnect*

Fig. 5. Processor and interconnect parameters of the ASM and values for two example targets (measured on Cell and estimated for a four-core SMP)

Parameter	Description	Cell	SMP
name	Unique name in platform namespace	'LS*n*'	'Mem'
size	Size, in bytes	262144	2147483648
clockRate	Clock rate, in GHz	3.2	0.4
latency	Access latency, in cycles	2	4
bandwidth	Bandwidth, in bytes per cycle	128	8

Fig. 6. Memory parameters of the ASM and values for two example targets

then messages have to wait, and are arbitrated using a first-come-first-served policy. There is a single unbounded queue per bus to hold the messages ready to be transmitted. The compiler statically allocates streams onto buses, but the choice of channel is made at runtime. The interfaceDuplex parameter defines for each resource; i.e. processor or memory, whether it can simultaneously read and write on different channels.

The bandwidth and latency of each channel is controlled using four parameters: the start latency (L), start cost (S), bandwidth (B), and finish cost (F). In transferring a message of size n bytes, the latency of the link is given by $L + S + \lfloor \frac{n}{B} \rfloor$ and the cost incurred on the link by $S + \lfloor \frac{n}{B} \rfloor + F$. This model is natural for distributed memory machines, and amounts to the assumption of cache-to-cache transfers on shared memory machines. Figure 7 shows the temporal behaviour of a single message transfer on a bus.

Hardware routing is controlled using the interfaceRouting parameter, which defines for each processor whether it can route messages from this interconnect: each entry can take the value storeAndForward, cutThrough or None. Memory controllers and routers are modelled as a degenerate type of processor.

Each memory is defined using the parameters shown in Fig. 6. The latency and bandwidth figures are currently unused in the model, but may be used by the compiler to refine the estimate of the run time of each task. The memory definitions are used to determine where to place communications buffers, and provide constraints on blocking factors.

5   ASM Program Description

The compiled stream program is a connected directed graph of tasks and point-to-point streams, as described in Sect. 3. All synchronization between tasks happens in the *acolib* communications primitives also described in that section.

The program model uses a trace, and the same trace can be reused for several different mappings of the program onto the target—as illustrated by the small feedback loop in the bottom right of Fig. 3. This reuse avoids recompiling the whole program via Mercurium and GCC, just to obtain a new trace. Because tasks may have complex irregular behaviour, the trace contains contral flow information inside the tasks.

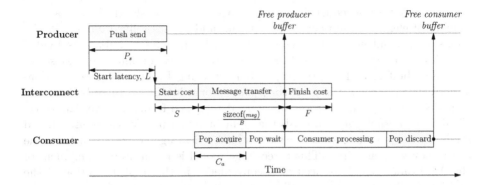

Fig. 7. Cost and latency of communication between tasks

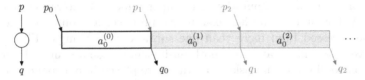

(a) Task containing a single subtask a_0; the superscript is the iteration number

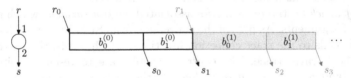

(b) Interpolation task containing subtasks b_0 and b_1

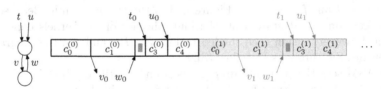

(c) Irregular task containing subtasks c_0, c_1, c_2, c_3 and c_4

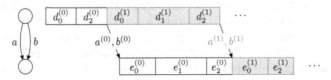

(d) Execution and communication of the program of Fig. 9 and Fig. 10

Fig. 8. Building tasks from subtasks

The basic unit of sequencing inside a task is the *subtask*, which pops a fixed number of elements from each input stream and pushes a fixed number of elements on each output stream. In detail, the work function for a subtask is divided into three consecutive phases. First, the *acquire phase* obtains the next set of full input buffers and empty output buffers, using ProducerAcquire and ConsumerAcquire. Second, the *processing phase* works locally on these buffers, and is modelled using a fixed processing time, determined from a Paraver [25] trace. Finally, the *release phase* discards the input buffers using ConsumerDiscard, and sends the output buffers using ProducerSend, releasing the buffers in the same order they were acquired. This three-stage model is not a deep requirement of the ASM, and was introduced as a convenience in the implementation of the simulator, since our compiler will naturally generate subtasks of this form.

A task is the concatenation of one or more subtasks. Figure 8(a), (b) and (c) show how to represent some tasks that perform an arbitrary fixed sequence of communication and computation. The superscript is the iteration number of the task. Although a stream has exactly one producer and one consumer task, it may be accessed from more than one subtask. For example, Fig. 8(b) has two subtasks, b_0 and b_1, and they both push elements on stream s. In order to support control flow, all subtasks of all tasks are placed into a common *control-flow hierarchy*. Subtasks are executed conditionally or repeatedly based on a Paraver trace attached to this control-flow hierarchy, with this common trace ensuring that communicating tasks behave consistently.

Each *if* or *while* statement has an associated *control variable*, which gives its sequence of arguments. As part of the conversion from SPM to C, the Mercurium tool inserts calls to the trace collection functions, which record the control variables in the Paraver trace. The control variables are represented using *event records* in the trace; the *event type* identifies the control variable, and the *event value* gives its value.

Figure 9(a) is the source code for an example stream program containing six kernels and an *if* statement. Figure 9(b) is the stream graph. Because the program contains an *if* statement, the multiplicities of the kernels depend on the data. However, within each shaded region, R_0, R_1, and R_2, the program is homogeneous Synchronous Dataflow (SDF).

The ASM sees the program after it has been partitioned. Imagine that the partition is as given in Fig. 10(a), so that task D contains kernels f1, f2, and g1, and task E contains kernels h1, k1, and k2. The tasks execute at the same frequency, but they both contain kernels from inside and outside the *if* statement. Conditional execution of g1 and h1, including modelling of computation times and their pushes and pops, is driven using a control variable in the trace.

Figure 10(c) is one way for the compiler to implement the given partition. The tasks are decomposed into subtasks, d0, d1, and d2, and e0, e1, and e2. Figure 10(b) shows the control flow hierarchy that controls the execution. The subtasks at the root are always executed, d1 is executed if the control variable is True, and e1 is executed if it is False. Figure 8(d) shows an execution trace where the decision values for this node are False, True, $\cdots$. The control variable attached to a *while* node is similar, but it counts the number of iterations of the loop.

```
1  #pragma acotes taskgroup
2  while (1)
3  {
4      #pragma acotes task output(a,t)
5      f1(&a, &t);
6      #pragma acotes task input(t) output(b)
7      b = f2(t);
8
9      if (cond)
10     {
11         #pragma acotes task input(a) \
12                             output(a)
13         a = g1(a);
14     }
15     else
16     {
17         #pragma acotes task input(b) \
18                             output(a,b)
19         h1(&a, &b);
20     }
21
22     #pragma acotes task input(a) output(u)
23     u = k1(a);
24     #pragma acotes task input(b,u)
25     k2(b, u);
26 }
```

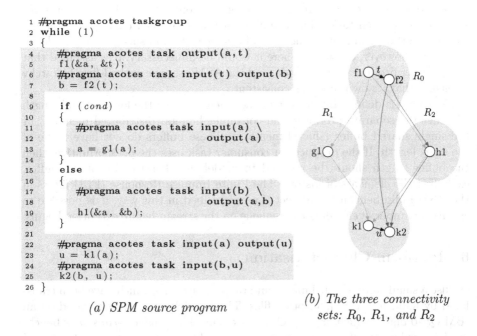

(a) SPM source program

(b) The three connectivity
sets: R_0, R_1, and R_2

Fig. 9. Example stream program with data-dependent flow

Task Kernels

D   f1, f2, g1

E   h1, k1, k2

(a) Partition

{d0, d2, e0, e2}

|
if
True /   \ False
{d1}   {e1}

(b) Control flow hierarchy

```
1  void D(void)
2  {
3      while (1)
4      {
5          f1(&a, &t);      // d0
6          b = f2(t);       // d0
7          if (cond)        // d1
8              a = g1(a);   // d1
9          push(s, a);      // d2
10         push(t, b);      // d2
11     }
12 }
13
14 void E(void)
15 {
16     while (1)
17     {
18         a = pop(s);      // e0
19         b = pop(t);      // e0
20         if (!cond)       // e1
21             h1(&a, &b);  // e1
22         u = k1(a);       // e2
23         k2(b, u);        // e2
24     }
25 }
```

(c) Extended C for partition

Fig. 10. Representation of data-dependent flow between tasks and subtasks

There are no explicit streams carrying the control variables of *if* or *while* statements between tasks. The compiler ensures that such tasks are consistent with each other, and may in the general case have to add such streams to do so. There are, however, examples where it would be unnecessary. It is assumed that the compiler produces correct code, and the ASM uses the control-flow hierarchy to ensure that its own model is consistent.

A stream is defined by the size of each element, and the location and length of either the separate producer and consumer buffers (distributed memory) or the single shared buffer (shared memory). These buffers do not have to be of the same length. If the producer or consumer task uses the peek primitive, then the buffer length should be reduced to model the effective size of the buffer, excluding the elements of history. The Finite Impulse Response (FIR) filters in the GNU radio benchmark of Sect. 7 are described in this way. It is possible to specify a number of elements to prequeue on the stream before execution begins.

6   Platform Characterisation

We use a small suite of benchmarks and target platforms, which have been translated by hand into the description files. The benchmarks were evaluated on an IBM QS20 blade, which has two Cell processors. The *producer-consumer* benchmark is used to determine basic parameters, and has two actors: a producer, and consumer, with two buffers at each end. The *chain* benchmark, is a linear pipeline of n tasks, and is used to characterize bus contention. The *chain2* benchmark is used to model latency and queue contention, and is a linear pipeline, similar to chain, but with an extra *cut* stream between the first and last tasks. The number of blocks in the consumer-side buffer on the cut stream is a parameter, c. For all benchmarks, the number of bytes per iteration is denoted b.

Figure 11 shows the time per iteration for *producer-consumer*, as a function of b. The discontinuity at $b = 16K$ is due to the overhead of programming two DMA transfers. For $b < 20.5K$, the bottleneck is the computation time of the producer task, as can be seen in Fig. 13(a) and (b), which compares real and simulated

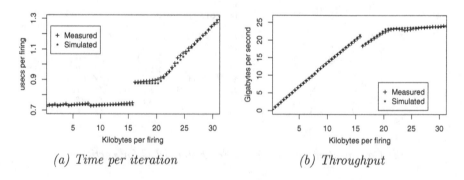

(a) *Time per iteration*   (b) *Throughput*

Fig. 11. Results for the producer-consumer benchmark

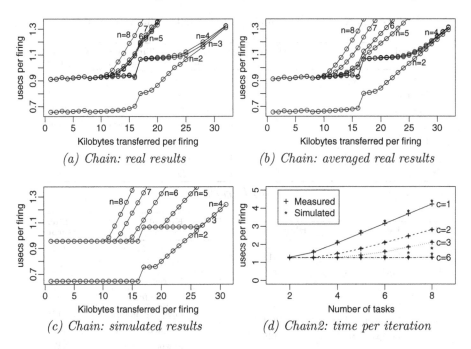

(a) *Chain: real results*   (b) *Chain: averaged real results*

(c) *Chain: simulated results*   (d) *Chain2: time per iteration*

Fig. 12. Time per iteration for the chain and chain2 benchmarks

traces for $b = 8K$. For $b > 20.5K$, the bottleneck is the interconnect, and the slope of the line is the reciprocal of the bandwidth: $25.6\,GB/s$. Figure 13(c) and (d) compares real and simulated traces for $b = 24K$. The maximum relative error for $0 < b < 32K$ is 3.1%.

Figure 12 shows the time per iteration for *chain*, as a function of n, the number of tasks, and b, the block size. Figure 12(a) shows the measured performance on the IBM QS20 blade, when tasks are allocated to SPEs in increasing numerical order. The EIB on the Cell processor consists of two clockwise and two anticlockwise rings, each supporting up to three simultaneous transfers provided that they do not overlap. The drop in real, measured, performance from $n = 4$ to $n = 5$ and from $n = 7$ to $n = 8$ is due to contention on certain hops of the EIB, which the ASM does not attempt to model. As described in Sect. 4, the ASM models an interconnect as a set of parallel buses. Figure 12(b) shows the average of the measured performance of three random permutations of the SPEs. The simulated results in Fig. 12(c) are hence close to the expected results, in a probabilistic sense, when the physical ordering of the SPEs is not known.

Figure 12(d) shows the time per iteration for *chain2*, as a function of the number of tasks, n, and the size of the consumer-side buffer of the *shortcut* stream between the first and last tasks, denoted c. The bottleneck is either the computation time of the first task ($1.27\,\mu s$ per iteration) or is due to the latency of the chain being exposed due to the finite length of the queue on the shortcut stream. Figure 13(e) and (f) shows real and simulated traces for the latter case, with $n = 7$ and $c = 2$.

Table 1. Kernels and mappings of the GNU radio benchmark

Kernel	Multiplicity	History buffer	Time per firing (us)	% of total load
Demodulation	8	n/a	398	1.7%
Lowpass (middle)	1	1.6K	7,220	3.8%
Bandpass	8	1.6K	7,246	30.4%
Carrier	8	3.2K	14,351	60.2%
Frequency shift	8	n/a	12	0.1%
Lowpass (side)	1	1.6K	7,361	3.9%
Sum	1	n/a	13	0.0%

(a) Kernels

Task	Kernel	Blocking factor
1	Demodulation	512
2	Lowpass (middle)	128
3	Bandpass	1024
4	Carrier	1024
5	Frequency shift	1024
6	Lowpass (side)	128
7	Sum	128

(b) Naive mapping

Task	Kernel	Blocking factor
1	Demodulation	1024
	Bandpass	1024
2	Carrier (even)	1024
3	Carrier (odd)	1024
4	Lowpass (middle)	128
	Frequency shift	1024
	Lowpass (side)	128
	Sum	128

(c) Optimized mapping

7   Validation

This section describes the validation work using our GNU radio benchmark, which is based on the FM stereo demodulator in GNU Radio [26]. Table 1(a) shows the computation time and multiplicity per kernel, the latter being the number of times it is executed per pair of l and r output elements. Four of the kernels, being FIR filters, peek backwards in the input stream, requiring history as indicated in the table. Other than this, all kernels are stateless.

Table 1 shows two mappings of the GNU radio benchmark onto the Cell B.E. The first allocates one task per kernel, using seven of the eight SPEs. Based on the resource utilization, the *Carrier* kernel was split into two worker tasks and the remaining kernels were partitioned onto two other SPEs. This gives 79% utilization of four processors, and approximately twice the throughput of the unoptimized mapping, at 7.71 ms per iteration, rather than 14.73 ms per iteration. The throughput and latency from the simulator are within 0.5% and 2% respectively.

8   Using the ASM

This section explains how the ACOTES stream compiler uses the ASM machine description and simulator.

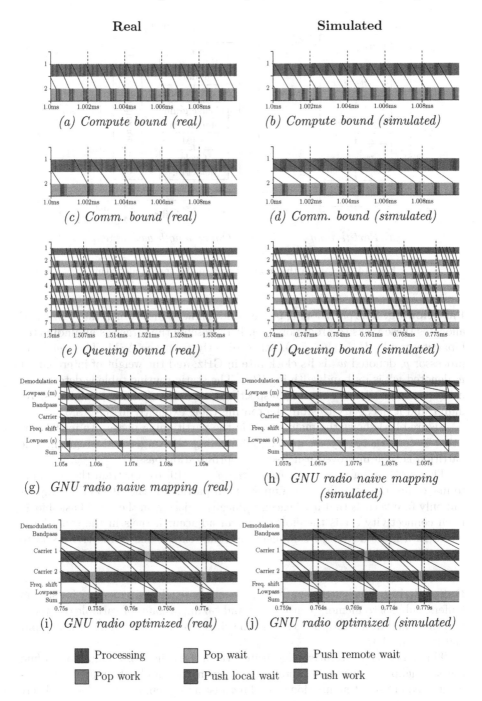

Fig. 13. Comparison of real and simulated traces

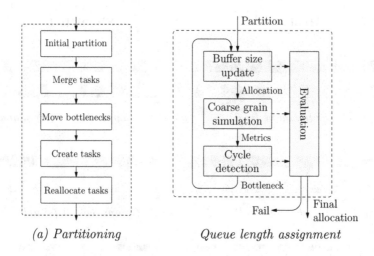

(a) Partitioning   *Queue length assignment*

Fig. 14. Detail on the main phases in the search algorithm

Partitioning. The partitioning phase decides how to fuse kernels into tasks, and allocates these tasks to processors [19]. It represents the target as an undirected bipartite graph, $H = (V_H, E_H)$, taken directly from the ASM. The weight of processor p, denoted w^p is its clock rate in GHz, and the weight of interconnect u, denoted w^u is its bandwidth in GB/s. The static routing table is determined using minimum distance routing, respecting the interfaceRouting parameters. We didn't find it necessary to store the routing table explicitly in the ASM.

Figure 14(a) shows the main stages in the partitioning phase. An initial partition is constructed by recursively subdividing the target and program. The partition is then improved using several optimization passes.

The partitioning phase uses *connectivity sets* [19] to constrain the mapping to make sure the compiler can support it. In particular, the ACOTES compiler can only fuse kernels that are lexicographically adjacent in the same basic block. Each connectivity set is therefore a pair of adjacent kernels in the same basic block. In a more advanced compiler, we would expect the connectivity sets to be as illustrated in Fig. 9(b).

Buffer Sizing. The queue length assignment phase allocates memory for stream buffers, subject to memory constraints, and taking account of variable computation times and task multiplicities [18]. The objectives are to maximise throughput and minimize latency.

This phase is an iterative algorithm, which uses the ASM simulator to find the throughput, utilization, and latency, given the candidate buffer sizes. As mentioned in Sect. 2, simulation is used because a mathematical model is unlikely to capture the real behaviour.

Figure 14(b) shows the main stages in the queue length assignment phase. A *cycle detection algorithm* uses statistics from the ASM simulator to find the bottleneck. There are two cycle detection algorithms: the *baseline* algorithm uses only the total wait time on each primitive on each stream, and the *token* algorithm tracks dependencies through tasks. The *buffer size update algorithm* chooses the initial buffer sizes, and adjusts them to resolve the bottleneck. The *evaluation algorithm* monitors progress and decides when to stop, choosing the buffer sizes that achieved the best performance-latency tradeoff.

The inputs to the queue length assignment phase are the stream program, minimum buffer sizes, and the *memory constraint graph*. The minimum buffer sizes can be one block, because an SPM stream program is acyclic. The memory constraint graph is a bipartite graph, $\mathcal{H} = (R_{\mathcal{H}}, E_{\mathcal{H}})$, where the vertices are the processors and memories, and the edges connect processors to their local memories. Figure 15 shows a memory constraint graph for the Cell B.E.

The memory constraint graph is generated from the addressSpace parameter for each processor. The remaining capacities are taken from the size parameters of the memories, *minus* the sizes of any code and data already in them.

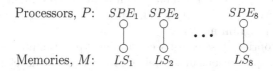

Fig. 15. Memory constraint graph for the Cell Broadband Engine

9   Related Work

Recent work on stream programming languages, most notably StreamIt [27] and Synchronous Data Flow (SDF) [28], has demonstrated how a compiler may potentially match the performance of hand-tuned sequential or multi-threaded code [29].

Most work on machine description languages for retargetable compilers has focused on describing the ISA and micro-architecture of a single processor. Among others, the languages ISP, LISA, and ADL may be used for simulation, and CODEGEN, BEG, BURG, nML [30], EXPRESSION [31], Maril and GCC's .md machine description are intended for code generation (see; e.g. [32]). The ASM describes the behaviour of the system in terms of that of its parts, and is designed to co-exist with these lower-level models.

The Stream Virtual Machine (SVM) is an intermediate representation of a stream program, which forms a common language between a high-level and low-level compiler [33,34]. Each kernel is given a linear computation cost function, comprised of a fixed overhead and a cost per stream element consumed. There is no model of irregular dataflow. The SVM architecture model is specific to graphics processors (GPUs), and characterizes the platform using a few parameters such as the bandwidth between local and global memory. The PCA

Machine Model [35], by the Morphware Forum, is an XML definition of a reconfigurable computing device, in terms of *resources*, which may be processors, DMA engines, memories and network links. The reconfigurable behaviour of a target is described using *ingredients* and *morphs*. Unlike the ASM, the PCA Machine Model describes the entire target, including low-level information about each processor's functional units and number of registers.

ORAS is a retargetable simulator for design-space exploration of stream-based dataflow architectures [36]. The target is defined by the *architecture instance*, which defines the hardware as a graph of architecture elements, similar to the resources of the ASM. The purpose is performance analysis rather than compilation, and the system is specified to a greater level of detail than the ASM.

Gordon et al. present a compiler for the StreamIt language targeting the Raw Architecture Workstation, and applying similar transformations to those discussed in this paper [37]. As the target is Raw, there is no general machine model similar to the ASM. The compiler uses simulated annealing to minimize the length, in cycles, of the critical path. Our approach has higher computational complexity in the compiler's cost model, but provides retargetability and greater flexibility in the program model.

Gedae is a proprietary stream-based graphical programming environment for signal processing applications in the defence industry. The developer specifies the mapping of the stream program onto the target, and the compiler generates the executable implementation [38]. There is no compiler search algorithm or cost model. A version of Gedae has been released for the Cell processor.

Kupriyanov et al. describe an architecture description language (ADL) for *weakly-programmable arrays* [39] of simple processors in a regular two-dimensional mesh.

10   Conclusions

This paper presents the Abstract Streaming Machine (ASM), which is the machine description used by the ACOTES stream compiler. The ACOTES stream compiler automatically partitions, blocks, and schedules a machine-independent stream program for best performance on a heterogeneous multi-processor system.

The ASM is implemented by a coarse grain model, driven by a reusable trace. We explain how the ASM is used by the partitioning and queue length assignment stages in the ACOTES compiler. We also give the machine descriptions for two targets: the Cell Broadband Engine and an SMP.

Acknowledgements. The researchers at BSC-UPC were supported by the Spanish Ministry of Science and Innovation (contract no. TIN2007-60625), the European Commission in the context of the ACOTES project (contract no. IST-34869) and the HiPEAC Network of Excellence (contract no. IST-004408). We would also like to acknowledge our partners in the ACOTES project for the insightful discussions on the topics presented in this paper.

References

1. Carpenter, P.M., Ramirez, A., Ayguade, E.: The abstract streaming machine: compile-time performance modelling of stream programs on heterogeneous multiprocessors. In: Bertels, K., Dimopoulos, N., Silvano, C., Wong, S. (eds.) SAMOS 2009. LNCS, vol. 5657, pp. 12–23. Springer, Heidelberg (2009). https://doi.org/10.1007/978-3-642-03138-0_3
2. Olukotun, K., Hammond, L.: The future of microprocessors. Queue **3**(7), 26–29 (2005)
3. Amdahl, G.: Validity of the single processor approach to achieving large scale computing capabilities. In: Proceedings of the 18–20 April 1967, Spring Joint Computer Conference, pp. 483–485. ACM, New York (1967)
4. Kumar, R., Tullsen, D., Jouppi, N., Ranganathan, P.: Heterogeneous chip multiprocessors. Computer **38**(11), 32–38 (2005)
5. Chaoui, J., et al.: OMAP: enabling multimedia applications in third generation (3G) wireless terminals. SWPA001 (2000)
6. Hirata, K., Goodacre, J.: ARM MPCore; the streamlined and scalable ARM11 processor core. In: ASP-DAC 2007: Proceedings of the 2007 Asia and South Pacific Design Automation Conference, pp. 747–748. IEEE Computer Society, Washington, DC (2007)
7. Intel: IXP2850 Network Processor: Hardware Reference Manual (2004)
8. Dutta, S., Jensen, R., Rieckmann, A.: Viper: a multiprocessor SOC for advanced set-top box and digital TV systems. In: IEEE Design & Test of Computers, pp. 21–31 (2001)
9. Artieri, A., Alto, V., Chesson, R., Hopkins, M., Rossi, M.: Nomadik open multimedia platform for next-generation mobile devices. STMicroelectronics Technical Article TA305 (2003)
10. ClearSpeed: CSX Processor Architecture (2005). http://www.clearspeed.com/docs/resources/ClearSpeed_Architecture_Whitepaper_Feb07v2.pdf
11. Chen, T., Raghavan, R., Dale, J., Iwata, E.: Cell Broadband Engine Architecture and its first implementation. IBM developerWorks (2005)
12. Asanovic, K., et al.: The landscape of parallel computing research: a view from Berkeley. Technical report UCB/EECS-2006-183, University of California, Berkeley (2006)
13. ACOTES IST-034869: Advanced Compiler Technologies for Embedded Streaming. http://www.hitech-projects.com/euprojects/ACOTES/
14. Munk, H., et al.: ACOTES project: advanced compiler technologies for embedded streaming. Int. J. Parallel Program. 1–54 (2010). https://doi.org/10.1007/s10766-010-0132-7
15. Carpenter, P., Rodenas, D., Martorell, X., Ramirez, A., Ayguadé, E.: A streaming machine description and programming model. In: Vassiliadis, S., Bereković, M., Hämäläinen, T.D. (eds.) SAMOS 2007. LNCS, vol. 4599, pp. 107–116. Springer, Heidelberg (2007). https://doi.org/10.1007/978-3-540-73625-7_13
16. ACOTES: IST ACOTES Project Deliverable D2.2 Report on Streaming Programming Model and Abstract Streaming Machine Description Final Version (2008)

17. Balart, J., Duran, A., Gonzalez, M., Martorell, X., Ayguade, E., Labarta, J.: Nanos Mercurium: a research compiler for OpenMP. In: Proceedings of the European Workshop on OpenMP, vol. 2004 (2004)

18. Carpenter, P.M., Ramirez, A., Ayguadé, E.: Buffer sizing for self-timed stream programs on heterogeneous distributed memory multiprocessors. In: Patt, Y.N., Foglia, P., Duesterwald, E., Faraboschi, P., Martorell, X. (eds.) HiPEAC 2010. LNCS, vol. 5952, pp. 96–110. Springer, Heidelberg (2010). https://doi.org/10.1007/978-3-642-11515-8_9

19. Carpenter, P.M., Ramirez, A., Ayguade, E.: Mapping stream programs onto heterogeneous multiprocessor systems. In: CASES 2009, pp. 57–66 (2009)

20. Fursin, G., Cohen, A.: Building a practical iterative interactive compiler. In: 1st Workshop on Statistical and Machine Learning Approaches Applied to Architectures and Compilation (SMART 2007) (2007)

21. Stephens, R.: A survey of stream processing. Acta Informatica 34(7), 491–541 (1997)

22. Kahn, G.: The semantics of a simple language for parallel processing. Inf. Process. 74, 471–475 (1974)

23. van der Wolf, P., de Kock, E., Henriksson, T., Kruijtzer, W., Essink, G.: Design and programming of embedded multiprocessors: an interface-centric approach. In: Proceedings of the 2nd IEEE/ACM/IFIP International Conference on Hardware/Software Codesign and System Synthesis, pp. 206–217 (2004)

24. Girona, S., Labarta, J., Badia, R.M.: Validation of dimemas communication model for MPI collective operations. In: Dongarra, J., Kacsuk, P., Podhorszki, N. (eds.) EuroPVM/MPI 2000. LNCS, vol. 1908, pp. 39–46. Springer, Heidelberg (2000). https://doi.org/10.1007/3-540-45255-9_9

25. CEPBA: PARAVER Performance Visualization and Analysis Tool. http://www.cepba.upc.edu/paraver/

26. GNU Radio. http://www.gnu.org/software/gnuradio/

27. Thies, W., Karczmarek, M., Amarasinghe, S.: StreamIt: a language for streaming applications. In: Horspool, R.N. (ed.) CC 2002. LNCS, vol. 2304, pp. 179–196. Springer, Heidelberg (2002). https://doi.org/10.1007/3-540-45937-5_14

28. Lee, E., Messerschmitt, D.: Synchronous data flow. Proc. IEEE 75(9), 1235–1245 (1987)

29. Gummaraju, J., Rosenblum, M.: Stream programming on general-purpose processors. In: Proceedings of MICRO 38, Barcelona, Spain, November 2005

30. Fauth, A., Van Praet, J., Freericks, M.: Describing instruction set processors using nML. In: Proceedings of the 1995 European Conference on Design and Test, 503 (1995)

31. Halambi, A., Grun, P., Ganesh, V., Khare, A., Dutt, N., Nicolau, A.: EXPRESSION: a language for architecture exploration through compiler/simulator retargetability. In: Proceedings of the Conference on Design, Automation and Test in Europe (1999)

32. Ramsey, N., Davidson, J., Fernandez, M.: Design principles for machine-description languages (1998). http://citeseerx.ist.psu.edu/viewdoc/summary?doi=10.1.1.128.204

33. Labonte, F., Mattson, P., Thies, W., Buck, I., Kozyrakis, C., Horowitz, M.: The stream virtual machine. In: Proceedings of PACT, pp. 267–277 (2004)

34. Mattson, P., Thies, W., Hammond, L., Vahey, M.: Streaming virtual machine specification 1.0. Technical report (2004). http://www.morphware.org

35. Mattson, P.: PCA Machine Model, 1.0. Technical report (2004)

36. Kienhuis, B.: Design Space Exploration of Stream-based Dataflow Architectures: Methods and Tools. Delft University of Technology, The Netherlands (1999)
37. Gordon, M., Thies, W., Amarasinghe, S.: Exploiting coarse-grained task, data, and pipeline parallelism in stream programs. In: Proceedings of ASPLOS 2006, pp. 151–162 (2006)
38. Lundgren, W., Barnes, K., Steed, J.: Gedae: auto coding to a virtual machine. In: Proceedings of HPEC (2004)
39. Kupriyanov, A., Hannig, F., Kissler, D., Teich, J., Schaffer, R., Merker, R.: An architecture description language for massively parallel processor architectures. In: Proceedings 9th ITG/GMM/GI Workshop, Methoden und Beschreibungssprachen zur Modellierung und Verifikation von Schaltungen und Systemen (2006)

Prototyping a Configurable Cache/Scratchpad Memory with Virtualized User-Level RDMA Capability

George Kalokerinos, Vassilis Papaefstathiou(✉), George Nikiforos,
Stamatis Kavadias, Xiaojun Yang, Dionisios Pnevmatikatos,
and Manolis Katevenis

Institute of Computer Science, FORTH, Heraklion, Crete, Greece
{papaef,pnevmati,kateveni}@ics.forth.gr

Abstract. We present the hardware design and implementation of a local memory system for individual processors inside future chip multiprocessors (CMP). Our memory system supports both implicit communication via caches, and explicit communication via directly accessible local ("scratchpad") memories and remote DMA (RDMA). We provide run-time configurability of the SRAM blocks that lie near each processor, so that portions of them operate as 2nd level (local) cache, while the rest operate as scratchpad. We also strive to merge the communication subsystems required by the cache and scratchpad into one integrated Network Interface (NI) and Cache Controller (CC), in order to economize on circuits. The processor interacts with the NI at user-level through virtualized command areas in scratchpad; the NI uses a similar access mechanism to provide efficient support for two hardware synchronization primitives: counters, and queues. We describe the NI design, the hardware cost, and the latencies of our FPGA-based prototype implementation that integrates four MicroBlaze processors, each with 64 KBytes of local SRAM, a crossbar NoC, and a DRAM controller. One-way, end-to-end, user-level communication completes within about 20 clock cycles for short transfer sizes.

1 Introduction

Memory hierarchies of modern multicore computing systems are based on one of the two dominant schemes – multi-level caches, or directly-addressable local "scratchpad" memories. Caches transparently decide on the placement of data, and use *coherence* to support communication, which is especially helpful in the case of *implicit* communication, i.e. the input data-set and/or the producer of data are not known in advance. However, caches lack determinism and make it hard for the software to explicitly control and optimize data transfers and locality in the cases when it can intelligently do so. Furthermore, coherent caches scale poorly to over hundreds of processors. Scratchpads are popular in embedded [1] and special purpose systems [9,10], because they offer predictable performance

© Springer-Verlag GmbH Germany, part of Springer Nature 2019
P. Stenström et al. (Eds.): Transactions on HiPEAC V, LNCS 11225, pp. 100–120, 2019.
https://doi.org/10.1007/978-3-662-58834-5_6

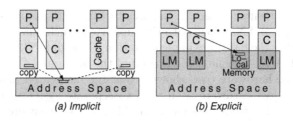

(a) Implicit   *(b) Explicit*

Fig. 1. Implicit vs. explicit communication

– suitable for real-time applications – and also offer scalable general-purpose performance by allowing explicit control and optimization of data placement and transfers. *Explicit* communication uses *remote direct memory accesses (RDMA)*; it is efficient, and it becomes possible in the cases when the producer knows who the consumers will be, or when the consumer knows its input data-set ahead of time. Recent advances in parallel programming and runtime systems [2, 7] allow the use of explicit communication with minimal burden to the programmers, who merely have to identify the input and output data sets of their tasks.

Our goal is to provide *unified* hardware support for *both implicit and explicit* communication within the same address space as shown in Fig. 1. To achieve low latency, we integrate our mechanisms close to the processor - in the upper cache levels, unlike traditional RDMA that is implemented at the I/O bus level. We provide *configurability* of the local SRAM blocks that lie next to each core, so that they operate either as cache or scratchpad, or as a dynamic mix of the two. Configurability is at *run-time* allowing different programs with different memory requirements to run on the same core, or even different stages of a program to adapt the underlying memory to their needs. We also strive to merge the hardware required by the cache and scratchpad into one *integrated* Network Interface (NI) and Cache Controller (CC), in order to economize on circuits.

We propose a simple, yet efficient, solution for cache/scratchpad configuration at run-time and a common NI that serves both cache and scratchpad communication requirements. The NI receives DMA commands and delivers completion notification in designated portions of the scratchpad memory. This allows the OS and runtime systems to allocate as many NI command buffers as desired per protection domain, thus effectively virtualizing the NI, while providing user-level access to its functions so as to drastically reduce latency. We improve SRAM utilization compared to traditional NIs (that used dedicated memories) by sharing the SRAM blocks between the processor and the NI, and we sustain high-throughput operation by organizing these SRAM blocks as a wide interleaved memory. The scratchpad space can be allocated inside the L1 or L2 caches and consequently the NI is brought very close to the processor, reducing latency. Our NI also offers fast messages, queues, and counters, as *synchronization* primitives, to support advanced interprocessor communication mechanisms. We assume *Global Virtual Addresses* and *Progressive Address Translation* [11].

This article presents, in Sect. 2, the architecture of the proposed integrated memory hierarchy and NI, along with the supported synchronization primitives. Section 3 describes the hardware implementation, through FPGA prototyping, of the configurable level-2 cache/scratchpad and the integrated CC/NI controller. We report on the hardware cost, showing that the merged NI and Cache Controller uses 35% less hardware than the two separate systems, in addition to the economy resulting from the shared SRAM space. We measure one-way, end-to-end, user-level communication to be about 20 clock cycles for short transfer sizes. We also evaluate the use of our primitives with software and present the performance benefits in a set of case studies, Sect. 4. Related work, conclusions, and future work appear at the end of the article.

2   Architecture Overview

Our proposed architecture targets chip multiprocessor systems with tens or hundreds of processor cores: each core has at least two levels of private caches and communicates with shared memory using Global Virtual Addresses [11]. This section describes run-time configuration of the local SRAM blocks as cache and/or scratchpad. We explain how scratchpad memory can be used to support virtualized NI command buffers, and present our hardware synchronization primitives.

2.1   Run-Time Configurable Scratchpad

Scratchpad space in our scheme is declared as a contiguous address range and corresponds to some cache lines that are pinned (locked) in a specific way of the cache, i.e. cache line replacement is not allowed to evict (replace) them.

Scratchpad areas can be allocated inside either L1 or the L2 caches. Most applications seem to require relatively large scratchpad sizes, so the L2 array is a more natural choice. Moreover, L2 caches offer higher degree of associativity, hence more interleaved banks. Although L2 latency is higher than L1, the performance loss due to this increased latency is partly compensated in two ways: (i) The L2 and scratchpad supports pipelined random accesses (read or writes) at a rate of 1 per clock cycle; (ii) configurable parts of the scratchpad space can be cacheable in the (write-through) L1 caches[1].

Owing to the use of progressive address translation [11], caches and scratchpad operate with virtual addresses, and the TLB only needs to be consulted when messages are transferred through the NI and the NoC to another node. In lieu of the processor-TLB, our architecture has a small table called Address Region Table (ART). As shown in Fig. 2, ART provides a few bits that determine whether an address region contains cacheable or directly-addressed (scratchpad)

---

[1] Write-back policy can also be used, provided that coherence between L1 and L2 is maintained. However, the write-through policy simplifies coherence without any performance loss. The inclusion property assumed here, is more intuitive than exclusion that would require moving locked lines between the cache levels.

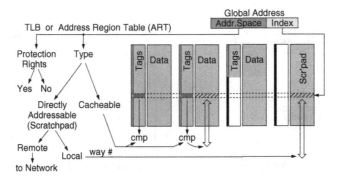

Fig. 2. Memory access flow

data. This is important when remote scratchpad regions are addressed, so that the hardware accesses them remotely, rather than locally caching them. It also obviates tag bit comparison to verify that a memory access actually hits into a scratchpad line; hence, tag bits of scratchpad areas are freed, and can be used for other purposes, such as implementing communication semantics for RDMA commands, counters, and queues that will be described shortly. Regions marked as local scratchpad in the ART occupy a set of blocks in the data portion of an L2 memory "way" block, such that low-order bits (the cache index) are compatible with the scratchpad address. The region can be freely allocated into any of the cache "ways", with ART identifying the "way" used. Each of the blocks in the region is marked as non-evictable in its state bits. This marking allows the distinction of memory access semantics at cache block granularity, and is used to ignore the actual tag-matching of the hit logic, as well as to prevent replacements. This mechanism allows for run-time configurable partitioning of the on-chip SRAM blocks between cache and scratchpad use, thus adapting to the needs of the application that is being run at each point in time.

2.2 Virtualized User-Level DMA

NI command buffers are DMA control areas which are allocated upon user software demand and reside in normal scratchpad regions. These buffers share the same ART entry with normal scratchpad and the distinction is made using a special bit (cache-line state), set upon allocation. Any user program can have dedicated NI command buffers (DMA registers) in its scratchpad region; this allows a low-cost virtualized DMA engine where every process/thread can have its own resources. To ensure protection of the virtualized resources, we also utilize permission bits in the ART and demand the OS/run-time system to update the ART appropriately on context switches. Moreover, the inherent support for dynamic number of DMAs at run-time promotes scalability and allows the processes to adapt their resources on the program's communication patterns that might differ among different stages of a program.

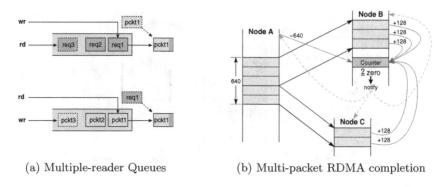

(a) Multiple-reader Queues   (b) Multi-packet RDMA completion

Fig. 3. Illustrating advanced interprocessor communication primitives.

DMAs are issued as a series of store instructions – to provide the arguments: opcode, size, source and destination address – destined to words within command buffers, that gradually fill DMA command descriptors, possibly out-of-order. The NI uses a command protocol to detect command completion and inform the DMA engine that a new command is present. All new and pending commands are kept in a *Network Job List* that is served by the NI according to its scheduling policy. When serving DMAs, the NI generates packets along with their customized lightweight headers. Packets belong to one of the two primitive categories: *Write* or *Read*. The NI carefully segments the DMAs into smaller packets when they exceed the maximum network packet size. The cache controller uses the *Network Job List* to request write-backs upon replacements and fills upon misses: the same mechanisms, and the same Read and Write packets, serve DMA transfers as well as cache operations.

2.3 Interprocessor Communication (IPC) Primitives

We provide advanced NI features that offer additional flexibility to the programmer in order to achieve more efficient communication between processors. We implement *Remote Stores* with write combining, to scratchpad regions of remote processors, in order to optimize remote access latency [15]; the ART can identify scratchpad ranges as remote. NI command buffers, described above, can also be used for fast *Messages*, allowing atomic, multi-word transfers. Message data are provided directly by the processor and no source address is needed. In addition, an explicit acknowledgment address can be specified to support software notification of transfer completion; acknowledgment addresses are allowed to be "null" to deactivate the mechanism. Multi-segment RDMA completion notification requires additional hardware support as described below.

We also provide *Remote Queues* as an appropriate level of abstraction for multiprocessor synchronization [4]. Queues are hosted inside scratchpad regions and their configuration (size, pointers and item granularity) can be programmed in the tags of special control lines. *Single Reader Queues* are provided to support efficient many-to-one control information exchange, with receiver polling

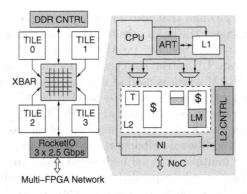

Fig. 4. FPGA prototype block diagram

to a single location. More advanced, *Multiple Reader Queues* (mr-Qs) are provided as a means for many-to-many synchronization, by allowing asynchronous write (enqueue) and read (dequeue) operations from any number of processors. As shown in Fig. 3a, read requests arriving at an empty mr-Q are recorded, waiting until corresponding writes arrive, thus effectively *matching* read and write requests in time. Upon successful matching, a response packet is generated; matching is dual, i.e. either writes or reads might wait to be matched. Multiple reader queues can also be used for locks or to accelerate task/job dispatching.

Finally, we implement *Counters* with atomic add-on-store capability, also hosted in scratchpad space, as a primitive to support completion notification for an unordered sequence of operations, such as multiple RDMA transfer completion, barriers, and other synchronization operations. Counters are initialized with a value (e.g total transfer size in bytes) via a remote store and trigger single-word writes to notification addresses when they expire (reach zero). For RDMA transfer completion, software can specify an explicit acknowledgment address targeting a counter, which will gather all partial acknowledgments for DMA segments, as illustrated in Fig. 3b. In the scenario shown, a single RDMA transfers 640 bytes. The destination region is mapped in the scratchpad of two separate nodes (nodes B and C). When all acknowledgments arrive at the counter, as well as the initialization value of -640, the counter triggers three notifications towards preconfigured addresses on nodes A, B and C. Counters is the only support required by the network interface for adaptive/multipath routing NoC optimizations, since RDMA transfer completion notifications will also work correctly with out-of-order packet arrivals. The only requirement for correct operation of the counter is that the NoC never generates duplicate packets.

3   FPGA-Based Prototype and Implementation

Our hardware prototype is implemented in a Xilinx Virtex-5 FPGA using four MicroBlaze soft-cores as processors. The processors are 32-bit, in-order, and have a traditional 5-stage pipeline that also supports single-precision floating point operations. Each processor tile has a private data cache hierarchy, with a configurable L2 cache/scratchpad memory tightly-coupled with our NI. Instructions are fetched from private L1 instruction caches. The prototype is equipped with a 256 MB DDR2 SDRAM which is used as main memory and is shared between tiles. Communication between tiles and the on-chip DRAM memory controller is achieved through a 64-bit, 5-port crossbar switch (XBAR) that features three priorities and applies round-robin scheduling; contention-less crossbar traversal costs 1 clock cycle. An additional switch port can be used to provide multi-FPGA connectivity through multiple external high-speed serial links (RocketIO), and thus our modular design can be expanded with multiple boards in order to build larger scale systems. Cache coherence is not currently supported. The operating clock frequency of the system is currently 75 MHz and its block diagram along with the major components is illustrated in Fig. 4.

3.1 Configurable Cache/Scratchpad Memory

Every tile of our prototype implements a private data L1 cache and a private, configurable, data L2 cache/scratchpad. These are smaller than one would expect in a CMP, due to limited FPGA resources. Typically, L1 caches range from 16 to 64 KBytes, 2 to 4 way set associative, with 64-byte lines. Our implementation has scaled down the L1 caches to 4 KB, direct-mapped, with 32-byte cache-lines. L1 caches are write-through, with 256-bit wide (one cache line) refills, a single-cycle hit latency, and follow "no-allocate" policy on store misses. L2 caches, on the other hand, are usually much larger, with sizes beyond 1 MB, associativity up to 16-ways, and line size of 64 bytes or more. Scaling down again, we have designed a 64 KB, 4-way set-associative write-back L2 cache with 32-byte lines. Our L2 cache supports multiple hits under a single miss in order to minimize processor idle time. The L2 controller serves write-backs and fills on misses, using the transfer primitives of the tightly-coupled NI as described below.

The key component that allows us to configure and use parts of the L2 cache as scratchpad is the Address Region Table (ART); its function is similar to a traditional TLB, but it provides only protection and type information – not physical address translation – hence the ART can be smaller than a TLB (and have no misses), because it can describe potentially huge regions of the address space in each entry. The ART classifies each memory access as one of: (i) cacheable, (ii) local scratchpad, (iii) remote scratchpad, (iv) tag access (used to access and set lock bits in L2), or (v) register access (NI control registers that customize specific features). The ART is placed in parallel with the L1 cache, and is probed on every memory access of the processor; a copy of the ART is also used by the incoming NI. Routing in our prototype is based on physical addresses, thus we use a static mapping: each L2 data and tag array has a unique physical address (nodeID and way number are encoded in the address bits).

An important issue for the efficient use of scratchpads and their associated DMAs is the available memory bandwidth. Scratchpad areas in our design are hosted inside the L2 memory banks and the NI accesses them at high rate

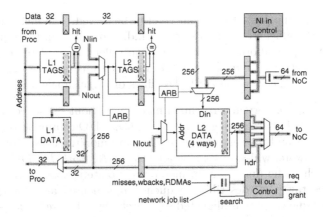

Fig. 5. Cache/scratchpad pipeline

when performing DMAs. On the other hand, the default set-associative cache organization would require all the ways (tags + data) to be probed in parallel, causing conflicts and thus limiting the available data array bandwidth for the NI. In order to reduce the bandwidth required by the typical L2 cache operation and use it more efficiently for NI operations, we implement a phased L2 cache: the tag arrays are accessed first and the data arrays are accessed only on hits. Our cache-line wide (256-bit) L2 data array, allows L1 misses to be served in a single clock cycle, thus we avoid occupying the data arrays for multiple cycles. The outgoing and incoming NI paths also access data in 256-bit chunks and since the NoC is 64-bit wide, the maximum access rate per path is 1 per 4 clock cycles. As a result, more than 50% of L2 cycles is guaranteed for L1 requests.

Figure 5 presents the datapath and the pipeline of our design. All memory accesses arriving from the processor are checked against the ART regions and probe the L1 cache. Hits are served normally, while misses, stores, scratchpad and tag accesses, are sent to L2 along with all required control information: type of access and way (if scratchpad). In the first cycle, the L2 controller arbitrates among requests from NI in, NI out and the L1, and probes the tags. In the next cycle, the selected agent accesses the data of a specific cache way. To reduce scratchpad access latency, scratchpad lines are L1-cacheable. The L2 controller keeps the cached scratchpad lines coherent by issuing local invalidations when writes arrive from remote nodes; no further coherence actions are required since the L1 is write-through. Scratchpad loads that miss in the L1, have a minimum latency of 4 clock cycles, while stores take 3 clock cycles to reach the L2. The observed processor latency for stores is 1 clock cycle, stores are immediately acknowledged and propagate in the pipelined memory hierarchy.

3.2 NI Operation and Mechanisms

The NI is tightly-coupled to the L2 cache and serves all transfers from/to the tile's memory and the NoC. The heart of the outgoing NI path is the *Network Job*

List which keeps the posted jobs that need to be served. The incoming NI path serves inbound traffic, stores data in-place and, depending on the type of traffic (cache or DMA), collaborates with the L2 controller to complete operations.

NI Command and Control Lines are allocated on software demand inside scratchpad areas, the state bits of locked lines distinguish them to four types:

- *Normal Memory:* normal scratchpad memory without side-effects.
- *Command Buffer:* are analogous to (virtualized) I/O command registers, and buffer RDMA and message requests. They are monitored by command completion hardware, which posts new jobs to the *Network Job List*.
- *Queue:* such cache lines contain metadata (pointers, size, item granularity) in the free tag part, describing a queue implemented as a circular buffer. The actual queue space is allocated separately, by software, inside scratchpad areas, outside the cache line itself. Two types of queues are supported: (i) *Single Reader Queues* (many-to-one) and (ii) *Multiple Reader Queues* (many-to-many). Single Reader Queues require one head and one tail pointer and the element size can be configured to 4-bytes, 8-bytes, 16-bytes, or a full scratchpad line. The head and tail pointers can be read via loads to specific block offsets. The Multiple Reader Queues have a fixed element size of 32-bytes and require one head pointer and two tail pointers: (i) a write-tail pointer for write packets (enqueues) and (ii) a read-tail pointer for read packets (dequeues). Incoming *write* packets (e.g. from remote store, message, or RDMA) destined to queue-type lines, are *enqueued* inside the circular buffer, and the NI controller updates the tail (or write-tail) pointer. Incoming *read* packets destined to Multiple Reader Queues record their response address in the queue body and update the read-tail pointer. Bound checking and pointer wrap-around is handled for head and tail pointers, as well as testing for queue full conditions. Matching a dequeue packet with an earlier enqueue packet (or vice-versa) is achieved by comparing the tail pointers with the head pointer and result in posting a new job in the *Network Job List*. The head pointer of Single Reader Queues is updated under software control while the head pointer of Multiple Reader Queues is updated by the NI when it completes the transfer associated with a *match* operation.
- *Counter:* these lines contain a 24-bit counter in the free tag part, and up to four notification addresses in the data part. Writes to word-offset zero increment the counter by the (signed) contents of the write. Upon reaching zero, the counter triggers the transmission of notification packets to the notification addresses by posting several jobs in the *Network Job List*.

Additionally, the NI serves incoming RDMA-Read requests. In order to meet the buffering requirements for incoming requests, without dedicating a separate memory block, we require the software to allocate a *Read Service Queue*, in the form of a Multiple Reader queue, and then assign its address to a special register.

NI Commands and Protocol: Commands to the NI are issued as a series of stores to the data part of Command Buffer lines. Our protocol defines two types of commands: *(i)* Copy and *(ii)* Message. Copy descriptors are DMAs and have a fixed size of four 32-bit words, while messages have any size up to one cache-line (eight 32-bit words in our prototype). In order to achieve automatic command completion, every descriptor should contain its own size (in bytes) inside the word at offset zero. The first word of every descriptor contains the following fields: *(i)* 8-bits descriptor size (bytes), *(ii)* 8-bit opcode (copy/message), *(iii)* 16-bit copy size (bytes - max 64 KBytes), used only when opcode is copy. For Copy descriptors this first word is followed by three mandatory virtual address arguments: *(a)* source, *(b)* destination, and *(c)* acknowledgment. For Message descriptors the first word is followed by two mandatory virtual address arguments – *(a)* destination and *(b)* acknowledgment – and up to five optional words that constitute the actual payload of the message. The NI uses its copy of the ART to distinguish local source addresses (write-RDMA) from remote sources addresses (read-RDMA), to validate (for protection purposes) the address arguments.

Completion Monitor: The NI includes a monitor circuit for command buffers, and uses the descriptor size to detect completion of commands, even in the presence of out-of-order stores, but assuming single-write of each word inside the command buffer line. The monitor is activated when stores arrive to cache-lines marked as command buffers, and a bitmap of the already completed words is formed and updated. The bitmap is kept in the free tag bits of these lines and when the number of consecutive "ones" matches those implied by the descriptor size, then command completion is triggered. Upon completion, a new job description containing the address of the command buffer is posted in the *Network Job List*. Since the completion bitmap is kept in the tags of each command buffer line, interleaved command issuing is supported offering full virtualization (e.g. threads can preempted while composing a command).

Remote Stores: Store instructions to addresses belonging to *remote scratchpad* regions (as identified by the ART), result in network packets carrying write requests, identical to RDMA or message packets (of data size 1 or more words). Stores marked as "remote" are kept in the *Remote Store Buffer*, and served by the outgoing NI engine as soon as it is free. A write-combining mechanism is implemented: if multiple remote stores to adjacent addresses arrive before some previous ones have departed, they are all coalesced in a single, multi-word-write packet. In order to support remote stores' completion notification, i.e. keep track if all remote stores have been successfully delivered, we use a special NI register that counts the total volume (in bytes) of departed remote store traffic; the acknowledgment address of remote store generated packets is automatically set to point to this register. Every time remote stores arrive in their destination(s), acknowledgment packet(s) that contain the delivered size are sent back to the sender in order to update the NI counter. The software can check the latter counter for *zero* to ensure that all remote stores have been successfully delivered.

Completion Notifications: We assume multi-path (adaptive) network routing, hence the multiple packets of a large RDMA may arrive out-of-order; the
packet data will be written in-place, given that each of them carries its own
destination address, but RDMA completion detection must now be performed
by counting the number of bytes that have arrived (our network never generates
duplicates). We implement counters to support RDMA completion notification.
Each *session*, of one or more RDMA operations, uses one counter (allocated
by software) as the acknowledgment address for its operations. The issuer decre-
ments that counter by the total size of all RDMA transfers. Every RDMA packet
carries the counter address in its acknowledgment field; upon successful write,
an acknowledgment is sent to the counter and increments it by the packet size.
When the counter reaches zero the NI automatically sends notification packets
to its pre-configured notification addresses.

Cache Transfer Support: The L2 cache controller issues requests for fills
and write-backs by posting new job descriptions in the *Network Job List*. The
job descriptions contain the appropriate opcodes and address: source address
for a fill and destination address for a write-back. The outgoing NI uses the
provided opcodes to format and generate the appropriate outgoing packets. The
cache controller uses a Miss Status Handling Register (MSHR) structure, to
keep track of outstanding write-backs and misses (transient cache-line states),
and updates it appropriately when the requests are served by the NI. The number
of supported outstanding cache misses is limited by the number of MSHRs; we
currently support one outstanding miss.

Outgoing NI: The outgoing NI engine features a *Network Job List* in order
to accept and manage requests for outgoing network operations. The sources of
requests are typically the following:

- *L2 Cache Controller:* requests for write-backs and fills.
- *Completion Monitor:* explicit transfers, i.e. RDMAs and messages, when com-
  mand completion is triggered for command buffers.
- *Counters:* up-to four completion notifications when a counter expires.
- *Multiple Reader Queues:* responses when enqueues and dequeues are matched.
- *Remote Store Buffer:* remote stores waiting in the remote store buffer.
- *Incoming NI engine:* remote acknowledgments from incoming packets.

Requests are posted in the *Network Job List* in the form of job descriptions.
Each job description contains: (i) an opcode field that specifies how the arguments are interpreted and how the transfer should be handled by the outgoing
NI engine, (ii) an address field that specifies either a local or a remote address
(it may be a cacheable address, a command buffer, an acknowledgment, or a
Multiple Reader Queue), (iii) the destination node number for the generated
packet(s), (iv) the network priority (three available) of the packet(s) in order to
avoid deadlocks of higher level protocols, e.g. cache coherence.

Upon receiving a job description, the outgoing NI first uses the destination node number to arbitrate for the NoC (request-grant protocol). When a network slot is granted the NI proceeds to the transfer, otherwise the current descriptor is recycled and put in the back of the *Network Job List*. The latter recycling tries to avoid head-of-line (HOL) blocking, when network destinations are congested, without requiring "expensive" per-output queues (VoQs). Recycling allows us to remove the outgoing per-priority network FIFOs, since pending transfers can wait inside the *Network Job List* and the packets need not be generated.

When a network slot is granted by the NoC, the NI operates in "cut-through" mode and generates packets – along with their customized lightweight headers and CRC checksums – that belong to one of the two primitive categories: *Write* or *Read*. Cache write-backs, RDMA writes, messages, remote stores and acknowledgments belong to the *Write* category (carry data payload and acknowledgment address), while cache fills, RDMA reads and remote loads belong to *Read* category (carry the request arguments). Orthogonally to the primitive category, the packets in our prototype are sent with different network priorities as follows:

- *Low priority:* cache fills, RDMA reads, remote loads.
- *Medium priority:* write-backs, RDMA writes, messages, remote stores.
- *High priority:* acknowledgments.

The payload of *Write* packets is acquired from the L2 data arrays, by iteratively reading chunks of 256-bits; the chunks are in turn serialized through the 64-bit NoC in four successive clock cycles. The NI segments large transfers, i.e. RDMA-Writes, into smaller packets when they exceed the maximum packet size (256-bytes in our prototype), or when alignment reasons dictate it. An RDMA transfer is served until it occupies a maximum network packet and then the corresponding job is recycled in the *Network Job List*; the associated command descriptor is also updated. Forcing large RDMA transfers to pause, offers fairness and reduces the latency of small packets that may wait behind large RDMAs. Moreover, the segmentation mechanism uses both source and destination addresses in order to generate packets that do not cross 256-byte boundaries. Additionally, our outgoing NI engine supports arbitrary source and destination address alignments (byte offsets) and leverages a barrel shifter to properly align and pad packets; the latter operation is only performed at the source nodes and thus the packets arrive to destinations nodes already aligned. When all packets of an RDMA transfer have been sent, the NI updates the actual command descriptor to signal local RDMA departure and allow the associated command buffer to be reused by software.

Incoming NI: The incoming NI exploits the header CRC contained in all packets and operates in "cut-through" mode to reduce latency. As soon as the header CRC is verified, i.e. destination address and packet size are correct, packets' payload can be safely delivered in memory without having to wait for body CRC verification; body CRC is carried in the last word of the packet. Upon reception, the NI writes the packets in per-priority network queues and notifies the

Table 1. Hardware cost breakdown in FPGA resources

Block	LUTs	Flip flops	BRAMs
MicroBlaze + Instr. Cache	2712	2338	4
L1 + ART	913	552	3
L2 Cntrl. + Arrays + Arb	1157	893	23
NI total	5364	2241	2
- Rem-Store Buff.	398	312	0
- Compl. Monitor	223	62	0
- Counters	286	99	0
- Queues	1011	45	0
- Outgoing NI	2042	1015	1
- Incoming NI	1404	708	1
Tile total	10146	6024	34
NoC (5 × 5)	2820	750	0
DDR2 SDRAM Cntrl	3745	4463	0
Total (4 × tile)	47149	29309	136

incoming engine; network priorities are strictly served in descending order. The incoming NI engine gathers up-to four 64-bits words from the incoming network queues in order to create 256-bit chunks and write them at once in the wide L2 memory. The engine has first to identify whether a packet belongs to cache or scratchpad traffic, by checking the state bits of the destination address. If the destination is a cache-line waiting to be filled, then the NI delivers data in place and signals the L2 controller; only write-type packets are supported for incoming cache traffic. Write-type packets destined to lines in scratchpad space have to perform different steps according to the type of the line. In plain scratchpad lines, data are delivered in-place and an extra write with the packet size is performed to the acknowledgment address, if non-NULL. All writes from the incoming network, generate local invalidations to the L1 cache to ensure that no stale scratchpad data remain there. Incoming write packets destined to *Counter* lines are handled in an analogous manner; only their first word is considered. If a packet is destined to a *Queue*, then the queue descriptor is accessed and the appropriate tail pointer (read-tail for read packets and write-tail for write packets) is used to enqueue the incoming packet. Read-type packets carrying a DMA request use the queuing steps, mentioned before, to enqueue in the *Read Service Queue*. Read DMA requests are handled as if they were Write DMA's from the local processor; however, a command buffer is fetched from the *Read Service Queue* pool, and a new job description is posted in the *Network Job List*.

4 Hardware Cost, Latency and Software Evaluation

This section reports on the implementation cost of our FPGA prototype, presents latency figures and evaluates software operations on top of our primitives. First, we report on the total area complexity of the prototype and then we compare plain cache and scratchpad designs against our integrated Cache/Scratchpad and NI. Finally, we illustrate the latency of the primitive operations supported by our NI and present some case studies with software evaluation.

4.1 Design Cost in FPGA Resources

Table 1 presents the hardware cost of the system blocks. The numbers refer to the implementation of the design in a Xilinx Virtex-5 FPGA (XUPV5-LX110T development board) with the back-end tools provided by Xilinx. The most complex block of our NI design is the Outgoing engine which serves jobs from the *Network Job List* and implements a low latency RDMA engine that supports arbitrary byte alignments and sophisticated packet segmentation. The outgoing NI engine costs approximately 40% of the total NI LUTs and 45% of the total NI Flip-Flops. The current total design occupies less that 65% of the available LUTs and Flip-Flops in our FPGA device, however we utilize 90% of the available memory blocks (BRAMs) and thus larger caches cannot be implemented.

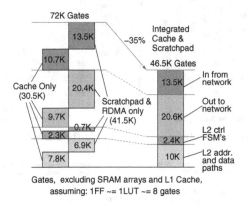

Fig. 6. Comparison of the area complexity for three separate designs: (i) cache only, (ii) scratchpad and RDMA-only and (iii) integrated cache and scratchpad.

4.2 Area Benefits of Integrated Cache/NI Controller

We have counted and report separately, in Fig. 6, the area complexity of three different designs: *(i)* all SRAM operating as cache only, and a cache controller; *(ii)* all SRAM operating as scratchpad only, and a NI providing DMA's; *(iii)* our configurable cache/scratchpad with its integrated NI/cache controller. The cache only design supports one outstanding miss, while serving hits under single miss, and does not support coherence. The scratchpad only design supports 8-byte aligned RDMAs and network packet segmentation.

The area here is reported in gates, to ease comparison, assuming that each LUT and each Flip-Flop is equivalent to 8 gates. The measurements do not include the L1 cache and the memory arrays. As seen, the integrated design *(iii)* has a complexity considerably lower than the sum of the complexities of the two dedicated designs, owing to several circuits being shared between the two functionalities. The circuit sharing is mostly observed on memory block datapath, the outgoing and incoming NI, and economizes 35% in hardware complexity.

4.3 End-to-End Latency

Figure 7(a) presents the latency breakdown of the following primitive NI operations: Remote-Store, Message and RDMA-Write transfers. The SW initiation cost, the NI transmit latency, the crossbar (XBAR) latency and the NI receive latency of every operation are constant under zero network-load conditions – both the outgoing and incoming path implement cut-through. The latency for the delivery of the packets' payload in the remote memory is commensurate to the size of the transfer.

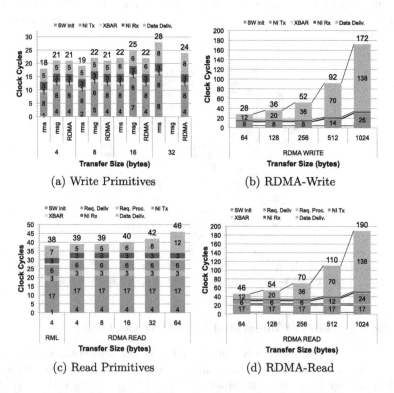

(a) Write Primitives   (b) RDMA-Write

(c) Read Primitives   (d) RDMA-Read

Fig. 7. Remote-Store, Message, RDMA-write, Remote-Load and RDMA-read transfers latency breakdown, as a function of data size (bytes)

Remote-Stores of 4-bytes cost 18 cycles and are faster than the equivalent messages and DMAs, since the initiation is implicit – no descriptor has to be posted. Minimum-sized messages and RDMAs of 4-bytes have the same end-to-end latency of 21 clock cycles. Although the RDMA has to read the payload from memory, and implies an extra memory access when compared with the case of a message, the outgoing NI manages to hide this extra latency during the NoC arbitration stage. For transfer sizes larger than 16-bytes RDMA achieves lower latency than remote stores and messages, however RDMA requires the packet payload to be already present in memory, thus is suitable for larger bulk transfers. The latency for large RDMAs is presented in Fig. 7(b) which shows that 64-bytes can be delivered remotely in just 28 clock cycles while 512-bytes cost only 92 clock cycles.

The NI transmit path has a latency of 8 clock cycles: 2 of them are attributed to the pipelined path to reach L2, 1 to enqueue a request in the network job-list, 1 for the outgoing NI to process the new request and 4 of them are spent on the NoC arbitration. The NoC request-grant phase takes 2 clock cycles but the granted network slot starts 2 clock cycles later – during that time the NI hides the latency of reading from memory and preparing packet headers. For transfer sizes that exceed the maximum network packet size, i.e. 256-bytes, and need to be segmented, an extra latency of 6 clock cycles is experienced per segment: 2 clock cycles are spent to recycle a request through the *Network Job List* and 4 clock cycles are spent again in NoC arbitration.

The NI receive path latency has two components: *(i)* the incoming cut-through latency and *(ii)* in-place delivery of packet's data in the memory. The incoming cut-through path has a latency of 3 clock cycles: 2 clock cycles are needed to receive the packet headers and check CRC and 1 clock cycle is needed to inform the incoming DMA engine about a new packet arrival. The incoming DMA engine, that delivers data in-place, needs 2 clock cycles to dequeue the packet headers from the incoming network queues and the remaining latency, until the last word is delivered in memory, is commensurate to the payload size. For 32-byte packets, 4 clock cycles are need to gather a 256-bit chunk and 2 additional clock cycles are needed in order to arbitrate for the tag and memory arrays. The memory arbitration latency is overlapped with the gathering of the next packet words and thus experienced only once per packet.

Figure 7(c and d) illustrates the latency breakdown of primitive remote read operations: Remote-Load and RDMA-Read. Besides the SW initiation cost, all remote read operations have a constant latency of delivering a request to a remote node which is 17 clock cycles – equal to delivering a packet of 8-bytes, contains the destination address for the source node. Thereafter, the request takes 3 clock cycles to be processed by the NI and be converted into an RDMA-write, as if it was initiated locally. The response latency follows the same steps with an RDMA-write and experiences the same latencies. Back at the initiator, the reception of a Remote-Load response takes an extra 2 clock cycles, when compared to and RDMA-Read, since the data should follow the L2 pipeline and be returned to the processor – RDMA-Reads are delivered in the L2/Scratchpad memory. A remote load of 4-bytes costs as low as 38 clock cycles while an RDMA -Read of the same size costs 39 clock cycles. Reading 64-bytes from a remote node costs just 46 clock cycles while reading 512-bytes takes 110 clock cycles.

4.4   Case Studies: Software Use of Hardware Primitives

This subsection focuses on the use of the proposed hardware primitives by software constructs and illustrates some common cases where our primitives find use. Apart from minimizing the latency of data transfers through virtualized low-latency RDMA and remote stores, software can use our primitives to efficiently implement higher level operations such as: (i) Transfer Completion Notification, (ii) Barrier, and (iii) Distributed and Centralized Task/Job Dispatching.

Table 2. Comparison of software-only operations vs. hardware-assisted.

Transfer Completion				Barrier			
size	clock cycles/iteration		improv.	cores	clock cycles/barrier		improv.
(bytes)	SW only	HW Cnt.	percent	#	Lock Based	HW Cnt.	factor
200	233	206	13%	1	111	41	2.7x
500	552	449	23%	2	194	66	2.9x
1000	1084	831	30%	3	357	78	4.5x
2000	2152	1620	33%	4	574	84	6.8x

Distributed Task Scheduling				Centralized Task Scheduling			
Masters	clock cycles/task		improv.	Masters	clock cycles/task		improv.
Workers	Lock Based	HW SRQ	factor	Workers	Lock Based	HW MRQ	factor
1M - 1W	199	40	4.9x	3M - 1W	232	87	2.6x
2M - 1W	152	40	3.8x	2M - 2W	237	44	5.3x
3M - 1W	151	40	3.8x	1M - 3W	270	35	7.7x

Transfer Completion Notification: We study a common scenario where a producer sends data to a consumer in pre-agreed buffer space that forms a circular queue. The consumer needs to know when all data have arrived and typically a software-built protocol manages the low-level details. The use of interrupts for the reception of packets at the consumer is prohibitive due to frequent context-switches (especially for small packets) and thus packet reception is typically triggered by checking a flag in the last word of the packet. The problem becomes harder when out-of-order networks come into picture and when the transfer size exceeds the maximum network packet size. The producer has to squeeze flags in the buffers to be transferred and the consumer needs to poll all these flags before arrival is triggered; additionally data are not contiguous in the buffer space since the flags have been injected. Our proposed solution is the use of *Counters* and the acknowledgment address offered by RDMA operations, Sect. 2.3. A counter per-buffer can be allocated at the consumer side and the producer can use its address as acknowledgment address when it issues RDMAs.

We measure the performance of these two sketched implementations in the FPGA prototype for a scenario where 10000 buffers are produced and sent with RDMA to a circular queue with 4 buffer slots at the consumer. For the measurements we vary the buffer size using the following values: (i) 200 bytes, (ii) 500 bytes, (iii) 1000 bytes and (iv) 2000 bytes; sizes beyond the maximum network packet size, i.e. 256-bytes, generate multiple RDMA segments. As illustrated in Table 2, the HW counter approach offers up-to 33% improvement over the software-only approach; the performance gains increase with the size of the transfer since the number of RDMA segments increases.

Barrier: It is a very common operation used by parallel programs to synchronize a number of parallel threads/tasks. The typical software implementation, for a few participating threads, involves a lock-protected memory location which is increased when each thread reaches the barrier; the last thread that reaches the barrier wakes-up all other waiting threads. In lieu of atomic instructions on MicroBlaze, we use an external hardware mutex module, provided by Xilinx, that is placed on the memory bus and allows *test-and-set (TAS) like* operations in a "fast" non-cacheable address space (SRAM). Using the hardware mutex module, we implement a sense-reversing centralized barrier.

The barrier implementation using the *Counter* primitive is straightforward: the counter is initialized with the number of threads (negative value) and each thread sets a local scratchpad address as notification address of the counter (up-to four supported). Upon reaching a barrier, increments to the counter are sent through remote stores. When the counter becomes zero, it triggers automatic notifications to the pre-configured notification addresses. Multiple counters can be chained (counter notifies counters) to create larger wake-up trees and thus support higher number of cores in a scalable manner [12].

We measure and compare in Table 2, the performance of the two implementations in an empty loop with 10000 back-to-back barriers, while varying the number of threads from 1 to 4. The HW counter is up-to 6.8 times faster than the equivalent lock based implementation on 4 cores.

Distributed and Centralized Task Dispatching: Spawning and dispatching tasks/jobs is crucial in parallel and distributed systems, thus we study two cases of task dispatching: *(i)* distributed and *(ii)* centralized. Case *(i)* refers to a set of masters which initiate tasks to specific workers (statically scheduled): each worker maintains a queue where multiple masters may enqueue tasks but only the owning worker may dequeue (many-to-one communication). Case *(ii)* refers to a central pool of tasks (queue) where multiple masters may enqueue and multiple workers may dequeue allowing for dynamic scheduling and load-balancing (many-to-many communication). The typical software implementation of *(i)* requires the masters to acquire a lock in order to enqueue a task and increase the tail pointer, while the worker may dequeue without acquiring a lock. However, in case *(ii)*, where multiple workers dequeue, a lock is also required to guard the head pointer. Our proposed solution for *(i)* is a *Single Reader Queue*

(SRQ) per worker and for *(ii)* a central *Multiple Reader Queue (MRQ)*; these primitives offer atomic enqueue and dequeue operations, Sect. 2.3.

We measure and compare the performance of the software-only vs. hardware assisted implementations is an program where each master spawns 10000 empty tasks. We vary the number of masters and workers accordingly and report the results in Table 2. For case *(i)* the lock based enqueue incurs an overhead which, for 1 master, cannot be amortized by the task size, whereas some of the overhead is overlapped with multiple masters. The SRQ implementation performs up-to 4.9 times faster and the number of masters does not influence the task processing time. In case *(ii)*, the lock contention increases the task processing time when multiple workers serve tasks from the central queue. On the other hand, the MRQ performs very well allowing for up-to 7.7 times faster processing of tasks.

5   Related Work

Configuration of memory blocks has been studied before in the Smart Memories [14] project, but from a VLSI perspective. They demonstrate that using their custom "mats", i.e. memory arrays and reconfigurable logic in the address and data paths, they are able to form a big variety of memory organizations: single-ported, direct-mapped structures, set-associative, multi-banked, local scratchpad memories or vector/stream register files. The TRIPS prototype [17] also implements memory array reconfiguration, but in very coarse granularity. They organize arrays into memory tiles (MTs), which include an on-chip network (OCN) router. Each MT may be configured as an L2 cache bank or as a scratchpad memory, by sending configuration commands across the OCN to a given MT.

Network interface (NI) placement in the memory hierarchy has been explored in the past. In 90's, the Alewife multiprocessor [13] explored an NI design on the L1 cache bus to exploit its efficiency for both coherent shared memory and message passing traffic. At about the same time, the Flash multiprocessor [8] was designed with the NI on the memory bus for the same purposes. Cost effectiveness of NI placement was evaluated assessing the efficiency of interprocessor communication (IPC) mechanisms. Mukherjee et al. [16] demonstrated highly efficient messaging IPC with a processor caching buffers of a coherent NI, placed on the memory bus. Streamline [5], an L2 cache-based message passing mechanism, is reported as the best performing in applications with regular communication patterns among a large collection of implicit and explicit mechanisms in [6]. Moreover, NI Address Translation was extensively studied in the past to allow user-level access, overcoming operating system overheads [3], and leverage DMA directly from the applications [8].

6   Conclusions and Future Work

The development of our FPGA prototype and the hardware cost analysis of the configurable cache/scratchpad memory with the integrated *Network Interface and Cache Controller* proves the feasibility of our approach and the existence of circuitry that is shared between the network interface and cache controller. Our implementation shows that the merged cache plus scratchpad uses 35% less hardware than the two separate systems. Moreover, bringing the NI close to the processor, at L2 level, has significant performance impact in the latency of NI operations: one-way, end-to-end, user-level communication completes within about 20 clock cycles for short transfer sizes. Additionally, the use of our primitives by software constructs offers important performance benefits in a set of case studies. We are working towards merging the NI functionality with more advanced cache features and directory-based coherence.

Acknowledgments. This work was supported by the European Commission in the context of the projects SARC (FP6 IP #27648) and UNiSIX (Marie-Curie #509595). We also thank, for their assistance in designing the architecture and developing the prototype: Dimitris Nikolopoulos, Alex Ramirez, Georgi Gaydadjiev, Spyros Lyberis, Christos Sotiriou, Dimitris Tsaliagos, and Michael Ligerakis.

References

1. Banakar, R., Steinke, S., Lee, B., Balakrishnan, M., Marwedel, P.: Scratchpad memory: a design alternative for cache on-chip memory in embedded systems. In: Proceedings of 10th International Symposium on HW/SW Codesign (CODES), Colorado (2002)
2. Bellens, P., Perez, J., Badia, R., Labarta, J.: CellSs: a programming model for the cell BE architecture. In: Proceedings of ACM/IEEE Conference on Supercomputing (SC), Tampa, Florida (2006)
3. Bhoedjang, R., Ruhl, T., Bal, H.: User-level network interface protocols. IEEE Comput. **31**(11), 53–60 (1998)
4. Brewer, E., Chong, F., Liu, L., Sharma, S., Kubiatowicz, J.: Remote queues: exposing message queues for optimization and atomicity. In: Proceedings of 7th ACM Symposium on Parallel Algorithms and Architectures (SPAA), St. Barbara (1995)
5. Byrd, G., Delagi, B.: Streamline: cache-based message passing in scalable multiprocessors. In: Proceedings of the International Conference on Parallel Processing (ICPP) (1991)
6. Byrd, G.T., Flynn, M.: Producer-consumer communication in distributed shared memory multiprocessors. Proc. IEEE **87**(3), 456–466 (1999)
7. Fatahalian, K., et al.: Sequoia: programming the memory hierarchy. In: Proceedings of ACM/IEEE Conference on Supercomputing (SC), Florida (2006)
8. Heinlein, J., Gharachorloo, K., Dresser, S., Gupta, A.: Integration of message passing and shared memory in the Stanford FLASH multiprocessor. ACM SIGOPS Oper. Syst. Rev. **28**(5), 38–50 (1994)
9. Kahle, J.A., Day, M.N., Hofstee, H.P., Johns, C.R., Maeurer, T.R., Shippy, D.: Introduction to the cell multiprocessor. IBM J. Res. Dev. **49**(4/5), 589–604 (2005)
10. Kapasi, U., et al.: Programmable stream processors. IEEE Comput. **36**(8), 54–62 (2003). https://doi.org/10.1109/MC.2003.1220582
11. Katevenis, M.: Interprocessor communication seen as load-store instruction generalization. In: The Future of Computing, Essays in Memory of Stamatis Vassiliadis, Delft, The Netherlands (2007)

12. Kavadias, S., Katevenis, M., Zampetakis, M., Nikolopoulos, D.: On-chip communication and synchronization with cache-integrated network interfaces. In: Proceedings of ACM International Conference on Computing Frontiers (CF 2010), Bertinoro, Italy (2010)

13. Kubiatowicz, J., Agarwal, A.: Anatomy of a message in the Alewife multiprocessor. In: Proceedings of the ACM International Conference on Supercomputing (ICS), Tokyo (1993)

14. Mai, K., Paaske, T., Jayasena, N., Ho, R., Dally, W., Horowitz, M.: Smart memories: a modular reconfigurable architecture. In: Proceedings of the 27th International Symposium on Computer Architecture (ISCA) (2000)

15. Markatos, E., Katevenis, M.: Telegraphos: high-performance networking for parallel processing on workstation clusters. In: Proceedings of the 2nd IEEE Symposium on High-Performance Computer Architecture (HPCA), San Jose, CA USA (1996)

16. Mukherjee, S., Falsafi, B., Hill, M., Wood, D.: Coherent network interfaces for fine-grain communication. In: Proceedings of the 23rd International Symposium on Computer Architecture (ISCA) (1996)

17. Sankaralingam, K., et al.: Distributed microarchitectural protocols in the TRIPS prototype processor. In: Proceedings of the IEEE/ACM International Symposium on Microarchitecture (MICRO) (2006)

A Dynamic Reconfigurable Super-VLIW Architecture for a Fault Tolerant Nanoscale Design

Ricardo Ferreira[1](✉) ⓘ, Cristoferson Bueno[1] ⓘ, Marcone Laure[1] ⓘ,
Monica Pereira[2](✉) ⓘ, and Luigi Carro[3] ⓘ

[1] Dep. de Informática, Universidade Federal de Viçosa,
Viçosa 36570-000, Brazil
ricardo@ufv.br
[2] Dep. de Informática, Universidade Federal do Rio Grande do Norte,
Natal 59078-970, Brazil
monicapereira@dimap.ufrn.br
[3] Instituto de Informática, Universidade Federal do Rio Grande do Sul,
Porto Alegre 91501-970, Brazil
carro@inf.ufrgs.br

Abstract. A new scenario emerges due to nanotechnologies that will enable very high integration at the limits or even beyond silicon. However, the fault rate, which is predicted to range from 1% up to 20% of all devices, could compromise the future of nanotechnologies. This work proposes a fault tolerant reconfigurable architecture that tolerates the high fault rates that are expected in future technologies, named Super-VLIW. The architecture consists of a reconfigurable unit tightly coupled to a MIPS processor. The reconfigurable unit is composed of a binary translation unit, a configuration cache, a reconfigurable coarse-grained array of heterogeneous functional units and an interconnection network. Reconfiguration is done at run-time, by translating the binary code, and no recompilation is needed. The interconnection network is based on a set of multistage networks. These networks provide a fault-tolerant communication between any pair of functional unit and from/to the MIPS register file. This work proposes a mechanism to dynamically allocate the available units to ensure parallel execution of basic operations, performing the placement and routing on a single step, which allows the correct interconnection of units even under huge fault rates. Moreover, the proposed architecture could scale to the future nanotechnologies even under a 15% fault rate.

1 Introduction

The scaling of CMOS technology brings a new scenario concerning reliability of devices. At nanoscale basis the wires and connections become more fragile and consequently more susceptible to break. Furthermore, due to the inherent variability and the imprecision of fabrication processes at this scale, a large number

© Springer-Verlag GmbH Germany, part of Springer Nature 2019
P. Stenström et al. (Eds.): Transactions on HiPEAC V, LNCS 11225, pp. 121–139, 2019.
https://doi.org/10.1007/978-3-662-58834-5_7

of manufacturing defects is predicted [1]. While the fault rates are well below 0.1% on current technologies, this number could increase to 20% at nanoscale basis [2]. At these fault rates, traditional static approaches such as triple modular redundancy (TMR) or even N-modular redundancy (N-MR) can be compromised, due to the fact that in the described scenario there is a high probability that the added redundancy will also fail.

In addition, there is a need for flexibility after fabrication to achieve high performance at low power levels. Coarse-Grained Reconfigurable Arrays (CGRA) could be an alternative, and several reconfigurable architectures have been proposed over the past 20 years [3–7]. However, a common characteristic shared among these architectures that make their usage prohibitive is the need of special compilers and tools required to select the part of the applications and modify the source code or binary code to be executed on the reconfigurable array. This totally breaks the software compatibility principle that users have become accustomed to.

The interconnection model is another important issue that must be addressed in CGRA designs. Architectures found in the literature are organized in three main topologies: the unidimensional model [4], the stripe model [5,6] and the mesh model [7]. The models have in common the need of design time tools and compilers to perform the placement and routing.

In this context, this work proposes a reconfigurable architecture called Super-VLIW. In this architecture several parallel/sequential computations are dynamically allocated over a large set of functional units, even in the presence of faults. This work differs from a traditional VLIW processor where all long instructions are built at compile time. To dynamically configure the architecture, a binary translation mechanism is used, so the binary software compatibility is ensured. The binary translation has been widely used by companies to encapsulate RISC instructions inside the x86's processors in the past 20 years, and an unquestionable advantage is the software compatibility.

This work also proposes the use of a set of Multistage Interconnection Networks (MINs) to send/receive values between the units and the processor register file. The model is logically similar to the unidimensional model, but could be physically implemented on two dimensional organizations as the stripe and the mesh models. In addition, and most important, the placement and routing is done at runtime. Therefore, no special tools or compilers are needed.

This work also provides further contributions on fault tolerant homogeneous MIN without extra resources due to a dynamic placement and routing step. In addition, we will show that a MIN could support a 15% fault rate allowing the scaling to reduce feature sizes such as nanoscale. Moreover, as it will be shown, a MIN can be flexible to offer a fault tolerant interconnection for a CGRA to dynamically speedup a MIPS processor.

This paper is organized as follows. Section 2 presents some related work. Section 3 gives some background concerning the multistage networks. Section 4 presents the proposed work with details about how the Super-VLIW architecture works. Section 5 demonstrates the experimental results. Finally, Sect. 6 draws conclusions and future works.

2   Related Work

Since the beginning of the computer industry the demand for even more performance has never stopped. Parallel computers or processors could meet this increasing demand. However, a parallel processor requires some kind of communication system to interconnect its internal units, memories, etc. Interconnections are one of the main issues on a parallel computer system. The communication is the factor that limits cost; performance: size; and power. There are many features to consider when choosing an interconnection: performance (latency and throughput), scalability, regular design, physical and cost constraints, reliability, and so on. As the system complexity and integration continues to increase, due to the advances in VLSI technology, it has become feasible to build parallel processors and systems consisting of hundreds or thousands of units. In a parallel reconfigurable coarse-grained architectures, as one proposed in [5], named Piperench, the interconnections could consume more than 50% of total area. In a fine grain fabric like a regular FPGA this situation is even worse, where connections can take up to 90% of the area of the chip [8,9]. A multistage interconnection network provides a cost-effective way to meet network scalability, high reliability, routability and regular design.

A MIN can have a compact and regular VLSI layout, as shown for a butterfly MIN [10]. Recently, a multilevel FPGA architecture (MFPGA) at circuit-switching mode has been proposed in [11], using a butterfly fat-tree multistage and tree interconnections. Experimental results show that the MFPGA has better area efficiency when compared to the traditional FPGA architectures based on island-style to map circuits at gate level. However, this approach is implemented at bit level (LUT-level), and it depends on a placement and routing developed at compile time. Our approach differs from the previous one in three aspects. First, we use coarse-grained units instead of LUTs, reducing the time overhead and the memory space required to configure the architecture. Second, interconnections are configured at runtime, thus no extra tools or special compilers are required. Finally in the interconnection model proposed in this work, the faults are taken into account and we will show that the proposed MINs provide fault tolerance allowing execution even at a 15% fault rate.

Although the MIN fault tolerance capability has been widely studied [12] during the 80's, this subject is still an important topic of research [13,14]. One approach consists in adding extra stages [12,13]. One extra stage provides fault tolerance for one switch failure in a MIN with Log N stages [12], and at least K extra stages will be needed to provide multiple fault tolerance to K switches failures [13]. Recently, a fault-tolerant routing for Fat Trees has been presented in [14]. The proposed routing has been implemented inside the switches and it is based on exclusion intervals over the destination address to forward the packets through the network.

In addition to an efficient interconnection network, the reconfigurable capability is another important issue that can ensure flexibility, low power, high performance and fault tolerance. In most approaches the interconnections are simplified by using regular and local topologies like meshes. However the price to pay is the complexity of the placement and routing steps, which should be done at compile time like in ADRES [7]. Recently, an approach has been presented [6], which is based on a Benes MIN that allows connections among any unit from one row to any unit in the previous/next rows. However, the applications have been manually mapped to evaluate this architecture. Recently, a reconfigurable cache architecture has been proposed that protects on-chip caches in high failure rate situations by using Benes network [15].

Our approach differs from the previous ones in several aspects. First, the placement and routing is done at runtime in a single step, even in presence of faults. No compilation is needed and the software compatibility is sustained. Each unit has a global ID, independent of row and column. A heterogeneous set of units is taken into account, and the architecture is flexible enough to allow a dynamic placement and routing. Moreover, all units can send/receive data to/from all units by using a global low cost interconnection model based on a set of MINs. In addition, a 2D layout of our architecture is feasible, as shown by the previous work on MIN layouts [10,11].

3   Multistage Networks

A multistage interconnection network (MIN) consists of a set of switch columns or stages, where each stage is connected to the previous and to the next one. The MIN shown in Fig. 1(a) is an Omega Network with Log N stages [16], where the interstage connection is a perfect-shuffle. There are three main classes of MINs: blocking, rearrangeable and non-blocking. A MIN is blocking when at least one input/output permutation assignment cannot be performed. These networks can be unique-path blocking or multiple-path blocking. A unique-path blocking MIN has only one path to connect a given input to a given output, as showing by the path between the input 1 to the output 2 in Fig. 1(a). A multiple-path blocking has more than one path to connect a given input to a given output, such as an Omega MIN plus extra stages. Each extra stage doubles the number of paths for each input/output pair. A multiple path Omega with one extra stage is shown in Fig. 1(b), where the input 1 has two paths to connect to the output 2. If there are M paths, the MIN supports M-1 single faults for a given input/output pair. However, since the M paths in a multiple path Omega are not distinct, a single fault may affect more than one input/output pair. For example, the inputs 1 and 5 share the same switch at the first stage in Fig. 2(a). If this switch fails both inputs are affected.

A rearrangeable MIN can perform any input/output permutation. However, the exiting paths may have to be rearranged by reprogramming the internal switches. Finally, a MIN is nonblocking if it can perform any input/output permutation, independent of the order in which the switches are programmed. However, even for rearrangeable MIN, most routing algorithms are static, and suppose to know a priori all input and output connection pairs [17]. Since in a dynamic context, the connection pairs should be processing in order, the previous algorithms cannot be applied.

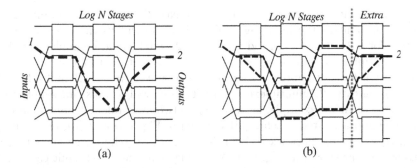

Fig. 1. Multistage interconnection networks: (a) omega network; (b) one extra stage omega.

Our approach is based on a dynamic placement and routing for a multiple path Omega, which is a blocking network. As will be shown later, the output selection is flexible, and when one output is unreachable (no path available), the placement will select another one preserving the existing paths. This approach is different from the rearrangeable routing algorithm because in the rearrangeable case instead of changing the input/output pair, the internal switches are reprogrammed when a path is blocking. In a worst case, all switches could be reprogrammed more than once for adding a new connection. Therefore, the rearrangeable approach is not feasible at runtime.

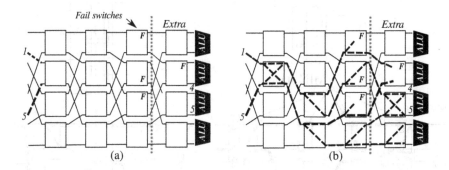

Fig. 2. Multistage interconnection networks: (a) shared multiple path and failed switches; (b) broadcast.

For example, let us consider a set of ALUs connected to MIN outputs as shown in Fig. 2(a), where all ALUs are available and some switch outputs are failed (F). Suppose that we intend to allocate the following computation $I_1 + I_5$. In our approach, a broadcast signal is sent to find the routable outputs even in presence of faults (see Fig. 2(b)). The first free and routable ALU will be selected. In this case, the third ALU is allocated, and input I_1 will be connected to output O_4 and I_5 to O_5, respectively.

Most fault tolerance approaches aim to increase the stage number, and/or the switch radix, and/or the interstage links. Figure 3 displays the internal switch structure for a 2×2 and 4×4 radix. The 2×2 switch could be implemented by two 2:1 multiplexers. Although, the 4×4 switch uses at least four 4:1 multiplexers, as a high level of approximation, if it is assumed that a 4:1 multiplexer is built by using three 2:1 multiplexers, a 4×4 switch will cost six times more than a 2×2 switch. As an example, let us consider two fault tolerant approaches, an extra-cube and a dilated-baseline MIN shown in Fig. 3(a) and (b), respectively. The extra stage cube network [12] consists of 2×2 switch Omega network plus an extra stage as shown in Fig. 3(a). Assuming that one switch fault can occur, three stages are added: one extra stage is added to duplicate the paths and two mux stages are added to bypass the first or the last stage. Observing the paths between the input/output pair 0 to 1, one can notice that there are two routing paths. If there is a fault at a single switch at the stage 2 or 1, as each path passes through two switches, the "healthy" switch can be used. However in case of a single fault at the first or the last stage, there is only one switch for both paths, therefore either the first stage or the last stage should be bypassed by using the mux stage. In case of multiple switch faults, some input/output pairs will be disconnected. This fault tolerant MIN has six stages, and it will cost the double of the single Omega MIN from Fig. 1(a), and it only provides a single fault tolerance. An extra-cube could be classified as a double modular redundancy (DMR).

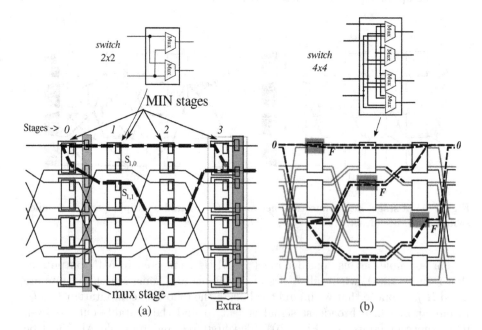

Fig. 3. Switch radix and fault tolerant min: (a) one extra stage omega; (b) dilated-baseline MIN.

Other approaches are based on high radix switches. Figure 3(b) displays a 2-dilated baseline MIN which has been proposed in [18]. This approach doubles the interstage interconnection and it uses 4×4 switches. There are n multiple paths for each input/output pair, as shown in Fig. 3(b) for the network input 0 and the network output 0. However, the multiple paths use a set of non-distinct switches. Considering $n = 8$, even for 8 multiple paths, only 3 faults would be enough to disconnect an input/output pair, as shown in Fig. 3(b), due to the multiple path share switches. The implementation cost could be six times more than a simple Omega MIN, as it is based on 4×4 switches. A 2-dilated could be classified as an N-modular redundancy.

3.1   Dynamic Placement and Routing

The focus of our work is to provide fault tolerance by using a runtime placement and routing for MIN. We previously described in [19] a dynamic placement and routing for MIN in a reconfigurable architecture [20]. MINs have been used in several domains over decades, since telephone networks at the 60's until high performance cluster computer comprised of thousands of processors. Instead of applying a MIN in a cluster with thousand of processors, we use a reconfigurable system with hundreds of simple functional units - reusing the very same basic idea at another level. The routing is embedded as a MIN structure, so it is easily scalable and it is not dependent on the interconnection pattern.

In this manuscript, the approach differs from previous work regarding fault tolerance. We extended our previous work [19] by including a fault tolerant routing. First, most works in fault-tolerant MIN [12] ensures that any input can reach any output even in the presence of faults. On the other hand, in our approach one can send the input to a different output performing an alternative path without affecting the correct operation of the architecture. Moreover, while in previous approaches the placement is done before the routing, and therefore the MIN should be fault tolerant on any input/output pair, we propose to compute the placement and the routing at the same time and during runtime, avoiding the need of pre-determined alternative paths.

Our approach is based on a previous work [19] where for each switch output, one local control logic has been implemented by using 2 bits, named as *busy* and *cross* bits. The *busy* signal is used to register if the output is busy or free. In case of busy, the *cross* bit stores the switch output configuration. There are two possibilities, one is a direct input connection ($cross = 0$) and another is a crossed input connection ($cross = 1$). Figure 4(a) displays some switch configurations and their configuration bits. A route request signal is injected in the MIN input as a broadcast signal to reach all MIN outputs. At each switch input, the route request will be sent to the output either if it is free (busy bit off) or busy but it could be reached if the cross bit had been configured in the same direction. In Fig. 4(b) the switch inputs and outputs are labeled by 0 and 1. Let us consider a MIN configuration (see Fig. 4(c)), where two connections between network inputs and outputs have been established, $I_1 \rightarrow O_2$ and $I_4 \rightarrow O_0$ as shown by bold lines. For easy of explanation, we uses the terms in_0, in_1, out_0, and out_1 to refer to local switch inputs and outputs, and I_i and O_j to refer to the network inputs and outputs. The switch is referred as S_{ij} where i is the line and j the column or stage. Assuming a broadcast signal from network input I_1, the local input in_0 at switch S_{32} will send a control signal to its outputs. As out_0 is free, it will propagate the control signal. Although the Out_1 is busy, it will also propagate to control signal, as it has been already connected to local input in_0 (cross bit is in the same direction). On the other hand, at switch S_{13} the in1 will send a control signal only to the out_0, which is free. The out_1 will not receive any signal from in_1, because it has been already connected to the other local input, which is the input in_0 instead the local input in_1. Therefore the *cross* bit is in opposite direction. The *cross* bit implements the multicast functionality when one input tries to connect to more than one output. We extend the control logic [19] by including an extra bit to register the faults. The control logic for the output out_0 will be as described in Eq. 1.

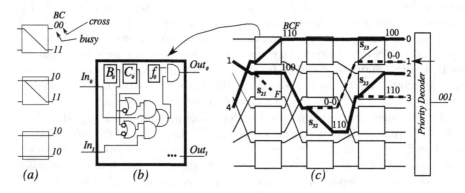

Fig. 4. Dynamic placement and routing: (a) some switch configurations; (b) switch local control logic; (c) a broadcast example.

$$Out_0 = (In_0(\overline{B_0} + C_0) + In_1(\overline{B_0} + \overline{C_0})) \cdot \overline{F_0} \qquad (1)$$

where In_0 and In_1 are the control inputs, C_0 and B_0 are the *cross* and *busy* bits, and finally F_0 is the fault bit for the output out_0, as shown in Fig. 4(b).

Let us consider a MIN configuration (see Fig. 4(c)), where two connections have been established, $I_1 \rightarrow O_2$ and $I_4 \rightarrow O_0$ as shown by bold lines. Let us consider also a faulty output Out_0 at S_{21}. Assuming that we want to connect the network input I_1 to another free network output. Starting by broadcasting a control signal from input I_1 as shown by a dotted line, the dynamic placement and routing will reach all free and routable outputs. At switch S_{21}, the output out_1 is faulty ($F_1 = 1$) and the control signal will be blocked, as shown by the **F** letter. On the other hand, although the Out_0 is occupied ($B_0 = 1$), it is a multicast case and the cross bit is set in right direction, then the control signal will be propagated through output Out_0. At the switch S_{32}, the output Out_0

is free ($B_0 = 0$), so it propagates the control signal, and the output Out_1 is a multicast case and the control signal is also propagated. Finally in the last stage, two switches will receive the route request. At S_{13}, the output Out_0 is occupied and the cross bit is set in opposite direction. However, the output Out_1 is free and routable, so this MIN output is reached. At S_{23}, the output Out_0 is also occupied, nevertheless it is a multicast case. Therefore the network output O_2 is routable. However, this MIN output has already been allocated. After the last stage, a MIN output vector is verified, where the busy outputs are set. At S_{23}, we have also the network output O_1, which is free, routable, and its entry in output vector is also free. Then, the first free output will be selected by using a priority encoder, which could be efficiently implemented by using lookahead techniques [21]. In this case, the MIN output O_1 is selected. In this approach, even under a high fault rate, the MIN will be able to connect some input/output pairs.

4 Super-VLIW Architecture

We propose here to redesign the topology to interconnect the functional units of the previous work [20] by using fault tolerance MINs. The new architecture model is called super-VLIW, which will be described in this section.

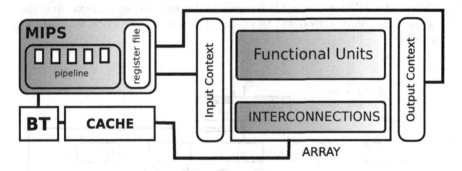

Fig. 5. Super-vliw architecture: a MIPS processor, a reconfigurable unit, a cache and a binary translation mechanism.

The reconfigurable architecture proposed in this work consists of a 5-Stage MIPS processor, a reconfigurable array (RA) of functional units (FU), a context cache and a binary translation unit (BT), as shown in Fig. 5. A dynamically reconfigurable architecture tightly coupled to a MIPS processor was previously proposed in [20], however the interconnection model presented in this work is based on buses and multiplexers. The architecture proposed here provides an area reduction by replacing the interconnection model with multistage networks. Furthermore, the fault tolerance approach proposed in this work also allows the use of the architecture in future technologies with high fault rates.

The BT is responsible for generating the instruction block (configuration) that will be executed on the reconfigurable architecture. It works in parallel with the MIPS' pipeline, hence there is no performance overhead to generate the configuration. Moreover, the BT dynamically transforms the sequence of instructions to be executed on the reconfigurable architecture without the need of instruction modification before execution, preserving the software compatibility.

To generate the instruction block, the first time the application is being executed on the processor, in parallel with the processor's pipeline the BT searches for instruction sequences that can be executed on the reconfigurable architecture. The second step is to analyze data dependency among the instructions to detect which ones will be executed in parallel or sequentially. Based on this analysis the BT generates the instruction block and stores in the context cache. All the steps since searching for instruction sequences until storing the instruction block are called detection phase. An instruction block consists of a super very long instruction word (super VLIW), and each block is stored in the context cache. The cache is indexed by the program counter (PC) of the first instruction of each block. Next time this PC is found the processor changes to a halt stage and the reconfigurable architecture starts the execution phase. In this phase the reconfigurable array is configured and the entire block is executed.

The configuration includes data copied from the MIPS register file to the input context, the interconnection setting and the unit configuration. Only the register values used by the current block will be copied. When the execution is finished, the MIPS register file is updated by the output context, and then either the next configuration will be executed or a new instruction sequence will be detected.

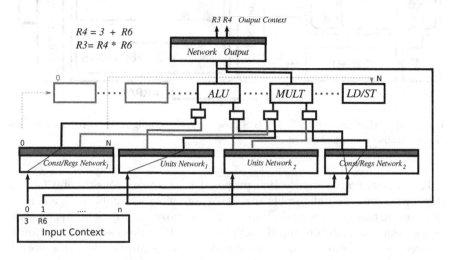

Fig. 6. Reconfigurable units and multistage interconnection networks

The reconfigurable array is composed of a set of functional units (FU), five interconnection networks, and input/output context as shown in Fig. 6. To provide an efficient interconnection a MIN must have the same number of inputs and outputs. However, since each FU has two inputs and only one output, and each input is able to connect to all outputs, the Super-VLIW interconnection system uses two separated unit networks for the left and right inputs, respectively. This approach does not increase neither the area nor delay as one $2N$-input network has the same cost of two N-input networks. The FU inputs should be connected to the input context to receive the register or immediate values. Thus, two separated networks are also needed. As an example, two instructions have been mapped in Fig. 6. The instruction $R_4 = 3 + R_6$ uses the register/immediate network on the left and on the right operands. As the second instruction, $R_3 = R_4 + R_6$, depends on the previous one, the unit network is used to route the result of first instruction (a forward connection). Moreover, as the right operand R6 is the same, a multicast connection will used on the right operand network. Finally, the FU outputs should be connected to the output context, so one more network is added. For the previous example, the output network will connect R_3 and R_4 to the output context. When a write-after-write (WAW) occurs inside an instruction block, only the last write operation is routed by the output network.

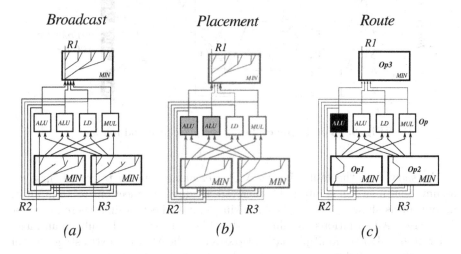

Fig. 7. An instruction placement and routing example.

During the detection phase, the binary translation algorithm will verify the instruction operands. Considering a three operand instruction $Op_3 = Op_1$ *op* Op_2, where Op_1 and Op_2 are the left and the right input operands, Op_3 is the destination operand, and op is the operation performed by the FU. When the binary translation selects an instruction to be executed on the reconfigurable array, the first step consists in sending a broadcast in parallel through the left and the right networks. The left (right) could be a register/immediate network or a unit network. At the same time, it sends a broadcast at the output context MIN from the Op_3 output. For ease of explanation, a simple example is illustrated in Fig. 7, which shows only two input networks. Suppose that we intend to allocate the instruction $Add\ R_1, R_2, R_3$. Each broadcast will find the reachable FUs of each operand. In our example, the operands 1 and 2 reach the ALUs and the multiplier (see Fig. 7(a)). However, only the ALUs are candidate to implement the ADD instruction. Finally, a bitwise AND of the three broadcast vectors is done, and a priority encoder will select the first reachable FU, which is the first ALU as shown in Fig. 7(c). The dynamic placement and routing is performed by the control logic network presented in previous section (see Fig. 4). Moreover, when the number of registers is smaller than the number of units, a register can be connected to more than one network outputs, which improves the routability of output context.

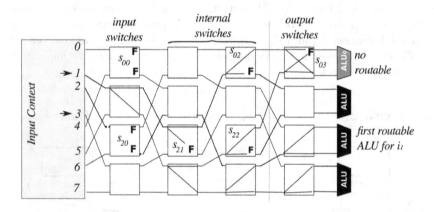

Fig. 8. Fault Tolerance during the placement and routing

To show how the faults in the MIN's elements can be tolerated, first we assume that a switch is internal if there are no direct connections to an input or an output as shown in Fig. 8. When a single fault affects a link, there are three fault cases. All situations are illustrated in Fig. 8. First, a link fault on an internal switch will affect multiple paths. However, if the MIN has extra stages, other paths will be available to connect some input/outputs. For instance, the connection from input 1 is affected by a fault at the switches S_{02}, S_{21} and S_{22}, although the routing could be done by selecting other paths. In the second case, a link fault occurs in an output switch, for example switch S_{03} and ALU_0. Therefore, this output will be unreachable. However, as the units are allocated dynamically, these affected units will behave as unavailable ones, and the allocation algorithm will avoid these units and search for the first routable unit available. Finally, when a link at first stage switch fails, as switches S_{00} and S_{20} shown in Fig. 8, only one of two inputs will be able to be used, and if both links fail, the two associate inputs will be disconnected. In this case, a register renaming approach is used to overcome the input faults. This approach is implemented by selecting the first available input, as shown in Fig. 8 where the first network input is I_1 and then I_3, since I_0 and I_2 are unavailable.

It is important to highlight that this work considers only permanent faults generated during the fabrication process. Thus, the information about the faulty units is generated before the binary translation unit starts, using classical testing techniques. In addition, no modification neither on the binary translation algorithm nor on the dynamic placement and routing are needed, and the solution to provide fault tolerance is transparent.

5   Experimental Results

To evaluate the performance degradation presented by the proposed architecture under different fault rates we consider as a reference value the performance of the 5-Stage MIPS processor, and all speedup results are relative to MIPS. Therefore, if the reconfigurable architecture generates a speedup factor of 2, this means that the proposed architecture is twice faster than the standalone MIPS processor.

As case study we analyzed three VLIW processors: a simple 8 units VLIW, a dynamic 8 units VLIW (called VLIW8) and a dynamic fault tolerant Super-VLIW. Both dynamic architectures are tightly coupled to a MIPS processor by using a binary translation mechanism. They differ in number of functional units and in the interconnection networks. The MiBench benchmark was used to evaluate the speedup of all approaches.

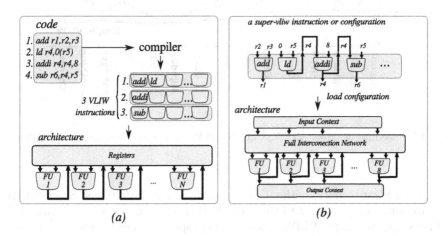

Fig. 9. A four instruction sequence mapped on simple VLIW and on VLIW8

The simple VLIW can only execute up to 8 operations (4 ALU, 3 Load/Store, 1 Multiplication) without any data dependence, and it works as a traditional

VLIW machine, as shown in Fig. 9(a). The source code is translated by a compiler
to a VLIW instruction without data dependences. For the binary code example
shown in Fig. 9(a), three VLIW instructions will be generated, and the execution
is done in three clock cycles. The dynamic VLIW8 processor has also eight FUs,
each FU has two full multiplexers and can connect to any input context or
FU using a non-blocking network. All FUs could receive register values or data
forwarding. As the interconnection is made by multiplexers, all interconnection
patterns are possible. The instruction block is built dynamically, and each block
can have up to 4 ALUs, 3 Load/Store units and 1 multiplier. In the best case,
all FUs will work in parallel, if there are no data dependences, while in the
worst case they will work sequentially. For instance, while the MIPS sequence
shown in Fig. 9(a) will be mapped on three simple VLIW words due to data
dependence, only one dynamic super-VLIW8 word is enough (see Fig. 9(b)).
The super-VLIW word stores the unit and interconnection configuration. As
mentioned before, this configuration is dynamically built on runtime. Finally,
the Super-VLIW has 128 FUs (90 ALU, 34 Load/Store and 4 Multipliers) that
are connected through the MIN networks as demonstrated in Fig. 6, targeting
parallel acceleration. Figure 10 presents the speedup achieved by each solution
when executing the applications from MiBench suite.

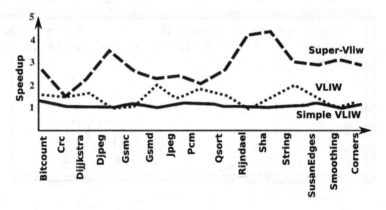

Fig. 10. Speedups of simple VLIW, VLIW8 and VLIW128 on the execution of MiBench
benchmarks.

On an ideal scenario without faults, as shown in Fig. 10, the Super-VLIW
can accelerate on average 2.84 times the MiBench benchmarks in comparison to
VLIW8 and the simple VLIW, whose average speedups are 1.7 and 1.17 respectively. Furthermore, if we consider only seven applications that show the higher
individual speedups, the Super-VLIW speedup increases to 3.4 times against
1.64 times for the VLIW8. Therefore, if the applications are more dataflow, the
Super-VLIW could be twice faster than VLIW8. The large number of units is
needed to capture larger block on the dataflow application.

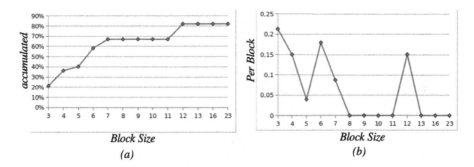

Fig. 11. PCM benchmark block size behavior: (a) accumulated histogram of execution time; (b) histogram of execution time per block size.

Each benchmark has its own behavior. As mentioned before, an instruction block is a set of instructions between two branches. For instance, Fig. 11(b) shows the histogram of execution time as a function of block size for the Pulse Code Modulation (PCM) benchmark. The large block has size 12 and it is responsible for 15% of the total execution time. However, the majority of execution times, around 70%, will be spent in small blocks (smaller than 7 instructions), as shown in Fig. 11(a). The execution time fraction displayed in Fig. 11 is relative to the execution phase. As mentioned before, first the block is executed in the MIPS, and in parallel the binary translator builds the reconfigurable block during the detection phase. Then, in the execution phase the block is fetched in the reconfigurable cache and runs on the reconfigurable array. This explains why the total accumulated time displayed in Fig. 11(a) is lower than 100%, because only the execution phase is taken into account. As the PCM is dominated by small blocks, the VLIW8 shows a performance close to the VLIW128 in Fig. 10. This is a control flow benchmark.

On the other hand, there are the dataflow benchmarks, as the Susan Edges (an image processing algorithm for edge detection), whose the block behavior is shown in Fig. 12. The majority of execution time is dominated for block sizes larger than 8 instructions (around 60%). Moreover, as speculative execution is performed by using two level branch predictor, the block size increases even more. There are some large blocks, 15% of execution time has the block size 169, and even the 128 units of our super-VLIW are not enough to capture the whole block parallelism.

Therefore, depending on the behavior of each application, the Super-VLIW can achieve a speedup significantly higher than the VLIW8 and in all cases the Super-VLIW speedup is always higher than the simple VLIW speedup.

Although the VLIW8 presented a mean speedup of 1.7 times in the execution of MiBench Benchmarks, the main problem of this solution is that it does not support faults. If a fault happens in any part of the multiplexer or the functional unit, it will invalidate the whole element. Therefore, in a more realistic scenario where faults must be considered the best solution is the Super-VLIW, since it ensures software execution even with several faulty FUs and interconnection units.

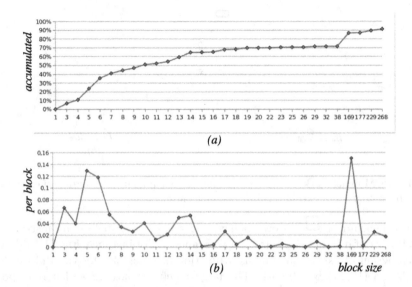

Fig. 12. Susan egdes benchmark block size behavior: (a) accumulated histogram of execution time; (b) histogram of execution time per block size.

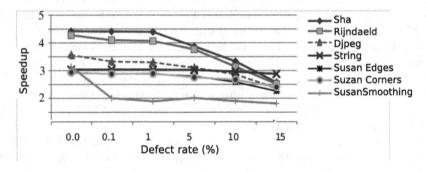

Fig. 13. The speedup degradation in presence of faults for the most significant MiBench benchmarks on the super-VLIW.

To evaluate performance degradation of Super-VLIW when faults affect the resources, the same benchmarks were executed considering different cases. Figure 13 presents an analysis of the speedup as a function of the fault rate. The graph presents the most significant speedups and five different fault rates were used.

As can be observed from Fig. 13, the Super-VLIW not only continues working even under a 15% fault rate, but also accelerates execution comparing to the standalone processor. According to the results, in the worst case, the average speedup is around 2.24 for 15% when executing all benchmarks from MiBench suite. Therefore, the Super-VLIW can be scaled to new technologies even in presence of faults.

Table 1 presents an analysis of the area as a function of technology scaling. Since the MIPS and the binary translation unit are critical to the correct function of the system, we have chosen not to scale them, as using larger feature sizes one could increase the reliability of the system. Hence, the size of both units at 90 nm technology will be $0.4\,mm^2$. Furthermore, the area of VLIW8 will be $0.6\,mm^2$, which is 3 times bigger than a single MIPS and the performance is only 1.7 times better.

On the other hand, the Super-VLIW can scale to new technologies that present higher fault rates. Since the functional units are less tolerant than the network, we can manufacture them in a larger feature size than the network. For example, the FU array can scale to $0.16\,mm^2$ at 32 nm, and the MIN size can scale to $0.03\,mm^2$ at 11 nm. The MIN will degrade the performance at 11 nm due to the high fault rate. However as demonstrated in Fig. 10, under 15% fault rate the average speedup is 2.24, and the area is around 2.4 times bigger than the single MIPS (0.53 for the Super-VLIW and 0.22 for the MIPS standalone).

Therefore, the speedup is proportional to the extra area. If the fault rate is lower, the speedup can be improved (up to 4.5 for some benchmarks as shown in Figs. 10 and 13). In these performance results we did not take into account the fact that as technology scales, the cycle time might shrink, and this means that one could expect further speedups by scaling the Super-VLIW.

Table 1. Estimated chip size according to the technology scaling (mm^2).

Technology	90 nm	32 nm	22 nm	18 nm	11 nm
MIPS	**0.22**	0.22	0.22	0.22	0.22
Binary translation	0.12	0.12	0.12	0.12	0.12
128 FU	1.3	0.16	0.16	0.16	0.16
MIN	1.8	0.23	0.11	0.07	0.03
Total area super-VLIW	3.5	0.73	0.61	0.57	**0.53**

6 Conclusions

This paper presented three main contributions. First it presented a reconfigurable Super-VLIW architecture with an online reconfiguration mechanism that also ensures software compatibility. The Super-VLIW uses a set of multistage interconnection network as interconnection model that was used to reduce interconnection costs. The second contribution corresponds to a dynamic placement and routing for the multistage interconnection network. Using the placement and routing as an atomic operation, one can dynamically find a path to a free functional unit even in the presence of a high number of faults. Furthermore, most works support at most a number of faults equal to the number of network stages $O(\log N)$. Our approach supports up to $O(N)$ switch faults. Finally, a fault tolerance approach to both reconfigurable architecture and interconnection model has been presented. The approach consists in avoiding the faulty functional units and interconnections.

We evaluated the system performance by using the MiBench suite. The analysis showed that our approach is still working even when the number of fault is 30 times bigger than the number of stages for a 128×128 MIN. The MIN network still works at 15% of fault rates. Therefore, we conclude that it is possible to scale the system to new technologies that present high fault rates, consequently the area overhead is significantly reduced by scaling the MIN. The entire system can be estimated to be 2.4 times bigger than a single MIPS and its performance is also improved by a factor of 2.4.

Acknowledgment. The authors would like to thank the following brazilian institutions for funding this project: Fapemig, CAPES, and CNPq.

References

1. Eshaghian-Wilner, M.: Bio-inspired and Nanoscale Integrated Computing. Wiley, Hoboken (2009)
2. DeHon, A., Naeimi, H.: Seven strategies for tolerating highly defective fabrication. IEEE Des. Test **22**(4), 306–315 (2005)
3. Hartenstein, R.: A decade of reconfigurable computing: a visionary retrospective. In: Proceedings of Conference on Design, Automation and Test in Europe, DATE 2001, pp. 642–649. IEEE Press, Piscataway (2001)
4. Compton, K., Hauck, S.: Automatic design of reconfigurable domain-specific flexible cores. IEEE Trans. Very Large Scale Integr. Syst. **16**(5), 493–503 (2008)
5. Schmit, H., Whelihan, D., Moe, M., Levine, B., Taylor, R.: PipeRench: a virtualized programmable datapath (2002)
6. Tanigawa, K., Zuyama, T., Uchida, T., Hironaka, T.: Exploring compact design on high throughput coarse grained reconfigurable architectures. In: 2008 International Conference on Field Programmable Logic and Applications, Heidelberg, pp. 543–546 (2008)
7. Mei, B., Vernalde, S., Verkest, D., Man, H.D., Lauwereins, R.: Exploiting loop-level parallelism on coarse-grained reconfigurable architectures using modulo scheduling. In: Proceedings of the Conference on Design, Automation and Test in Europe, DATE 2003, p. 10296. IEEE Computer Society, Washington (2003)
8. DeHon, A.: Balancing interconnect and computation in a reconfigurable computing array (or, why you don't really want 100 In: Proceedings of the 1999 ACM/SIGDA Seventh International Symposium on Field Programmable Gate Arrays, FPGA 1999. ACM, New York (1999)
9. Xilinx: The Programmable Logic Data Book 2003. Xilinx Inc., San Jose (2003)
10. DeHon, A.: Compact, multilayer layout for butterfly fat-tree. In: Proceedings of Twelfth ACM Symposium on Parallel Algorithms and Architectures, SPAA 2000, pp. 206–215. ACM, New York (2000)
11. Zied, M., Hayder, M., Emna, A., Habib, M.: Efficient tree topology for FPGA interconnect network. In: Proceedings of the 18th ACM Great Lakes Symposium on VLSI, GLSVLSI 2008, pp. 321–326. ACM, New York (2008)
12. Adams, G.B., Agrawal, D.P., Siegel, H.J.: A survey and comparison of fault-tolerant multistage interconnection networks. In: IEEE Interconnection Networks for High-Performance Parallel Computers, pp. 654–667 (1994)

13. Fan, C.C., Bruck, J.: Tolerating multiple faults in multistage interconnection networks with minimal extra stages. IEEE Trans. Comput. **49**(9), 998–1004 (2000)
14. Requena, C.G., Requena, M.G., Rodríguez, P.L., Duato, J.F.: FT2EI: a dynamic fault-tolerant routing methodology for fat trees with exclusion intervals. IEEE Trans. Parallel Distrib. Syst. **20**(6), 802–817 (2009)
15. Ansari, A., Gupta, S., Feng, S., Mahlke, S.: ZerehCache: armoring cache architectures in high defect density technologies. In: Proceedings of the 42nd Annual IEEE/ACM International Symposium on Microarchitecture, MICRO 42, pp. 100–110. ACM, New York (2009)
16. Lawrie, D.H.: Access and alignment of data in an array processor. IEEE Trans. Comput. **24**(12), 1145–1155 (1975)
17. Feng, T.Y., Seo, S.W.: A new routing algorithm for a class of rearrangeable networks. IEEE Trans. Comput. **43**(11), 1270–1280 (1994)
18. Kamiura, N., Kodera, T., Matsui, N.: Fault tolerant multistage interconnection networks with widely dispersed paths. In: Asian Test Symposium (2000)
19. Ferreira, R., Laure, M., Beck, A., Lo, T., Rutzig, M., Carro, L.: A low cost and adaptable routing network for reconfigurable systems. In: IEEE Reconfigurable Architecture Workshop RAW (2009)
20. Beck, A.C.S., Rutzig, M.B., Gaydadjiev, G.N., Carro, L.: Transparent reconfigurable acceleration for heterogeneous embedded applications. In: Proceedings of Design, Automation and Test in Europe (DATE 2008) (2008)
21. Mohan, N., Fung, W., Sachdev, M.: Low power priority encoder and multiple match detection circuit for ternary content addressable memory. In: Advanced International Conference on Telecommunications AICT (2006)

Author Index

Ayguade, Eduard   79

Bachmann, Christian   59
Bekooij, Marco J. G.   39
Bijlsma, Tjerk   39
Bueno, Cristoferson   121

Carpenter, Paul M.   79
Carro, Luigi   121

de La Lama, Carlos S.   21
Dutta, Hritam   1

Ferreira, Ricardo   121

Genser, Andreas   59

Haid, Josef   59
Hannig, Frank   1

Jääskeläinen, Pekka   21

Kalokerinos, George   100
Katevenis, Manolis   100

Kavadias, Stamatis   100
Kultala, Heikki   21

Laure, Marcone   121

Membarth, Richard   1

Nikiforos, George   100

Papaefstathiou, Vassilis   100
Pereira, Monica   121
Pnevmatikatos, Dionisios   100

Ramirez, Alex   79

Smit, Gerard J. M.   39
Steger, Christian   59

Takala, Jarmo   21
Teich, Jürgen   1

Weiss, Reinhold   59

Yang, Xiaojun   100

Printed in the United States
By Bookmasters